White Sea

FINLAND

● Novgorod

PRINCIPALITY OF RUSSIA

Caspian
Sea
KHAZAR
KHANATE

·ka ●

EDEN

Baltic
Sea

Kiev ●

POLAND

Black Sea

HUNGARY

Hedeby

·stad

GERMANY

Byzantium ●

BYZANTINE EMPIRE

Rome ●

Mediterranean Sea

ISLAMIC CALIPHATES

ISLAMIC CALIPHATES

The Vikings
and their
predecessors

by Kate Gordon
with a contribution by
Robert McGhee

National Museum of Man
National Museums of Canada,
Ottawa

Museum of Science and Industry,
Chicago

©National Museums of Canada 1981

National Museum of Man
National Museums of Canada
Ottawa, Canada K1A 0M8

Photographs © Statens Historiska
Museum 1981

Catalogue No. NM92-82/1981E

ISBN 0-660-10751-1

Édition française
Les Vikings et leurs prédécesseurs
ISBN 0-660-90270-2

Coordination
Madeleine Choquette-Delvaux

Editor
Charis Wahl

Design
BB&H Graphic Communications
Limited

Line Drawings
Jane Elston

Maps
James MacLeod
Jane Elston

Production
James MacLeod
Donald Matheson

Typesetting
Nancy Poirier Typesetting

Printing
Métropole Litho Inc.

This catalogue has been prepared to accompany the travelling exhibition of the Statens Historiska Museum of Stockholm, Sweden, "The Vikings and Their Predecessors," presented at the National Museum of Man, Ottawa from 16 December 1981 to 7 February 1982, and at the Museum of Science and Industry, Chicago from 26 February to 9 May 1982.

Printed in Canada

Contents

Foreword

Almost a thousand years ago, the crew of a Viking ship, storm-driven far west of their course, sailed out of the fog and sighted the eastern coast of North America. Although they did not land on the new continent, their reports led to exploration, the establishment of the short-lived Vinland colonies, and an historical link between Scandinavia and the New World.

The present exhibition furthers this connection by presenting to North American audiences a glimpse of the Viking world and that of their ancestors. Its aim is to broaden our view of their vital way of life by placing the Viking phenomenon in its historical and cultural context. When this is done, we see the Vikings, not as marauders suddenly appearing out of the mists of northern Europe in the eighth century, but as an integral part of European cultural growth during the first millenium A.D. Absorbing ideas and techniques from their southern neighbours, and adding these to their own rich heritage and inventive skills, the Scandinavian Norse gradually grew, not only as a military power, but also as a political, mercantile, and artistic force.

This international exhibition, the first to present the history of the Vikings in such depth, was assembled by the Statens Historiska Museum (Museum of National Antiquities) in Stockholm. We are very grateful to that museum, and to the people of Sweden for sharing with us their national treasures. The catalogue, prepared by scholars in the United States and Canada, is the first to be published jointly by our two museums. We should like to take this opportunity to thank all the people in Sweden, Canada, and the United States who have worked to make this exhibition a success. Their efforts are a fitting tribute to the heritage of the Vikings and to their far-ranging voyaging to destinations as distant as Byzantium and Newfoundland. It is with great pleasure that we welcome this exhibition to North America.

Victor J. Danilov
President and Director
Museum of Science and Industry
Chicago, U.S.A.

William E. Taylor, Jr.
Director, National Museum
of Man
National Museums of Canada
Ottawa, Canada

The Historical Background

In this year terrible portents appeared over Northumbria . . . fiery dragons were seen flying in the air. A great famine soon followed these signs; and a little after that . . . the harrying of the heathen miserably destroyed God's church in Lindisfarne by rapine and slaughter.

These words from the Anglo-Saxon chronicle for the year 793 helped to create our image of the Vikings as fierce warriors leaping from dragon-prowed ships to ravage the countryside. For almost three hundred years from about 800 to 1050, Vikings are said to have terrorized northern Europe. Yet a closer look reveals a very different picture.

The Vikings belonged to one of three ethnic groups living in what is now Denmark, Finland, Norway, and Sweden. The Lapps lived in the regions of Norway and Sweden north of the Arctic Circle. They hunted and herded reindeer, and their distinctive language and way of life have survived to the present day. The Finns speak a language related to that of the Lapps; they settled in what is now Finland, many centuries before their name was given to the country. The third group, the Vikings or Norsemen, lived in what is now Denmark, southern Norway and Sweden, parts of southwestern Finland, and the Baltic Islands of Bornholm, Gotland, and Öland.

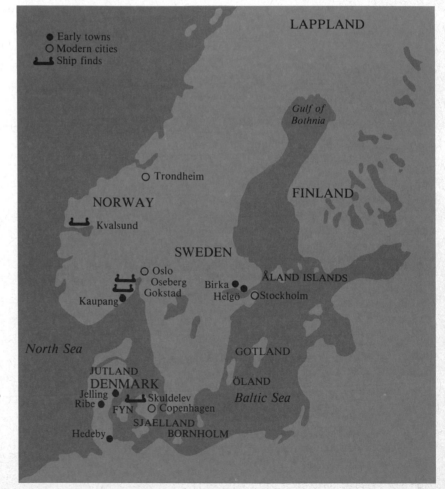

Norse culture was quite different from those of the Lapps, the Finns, and the Baltic and Slavic tribes that lived to the southeast of the Baltic Sea. Culturally and linguistically, the Vikings were Germanic – that is, related to groups living immediately to the south of Scandinavia, in what is now Germany. (Other contemporary linguistic and cultural groups included the Slavic tribes of Eastern Europe and the Celtic peoples of northern Spain, France, and the British Isles.)

The earliest inhabitants of Scandinavia were stone-age hunters, wandering tribesmen who followed the seasonal migrations of the animals they hunted. As the glaciers of the last Ice Age melted away, more than ten thousand years ago, the habitat of the animals moved gradually northward, and the hunters followed.

Between four and five thousand years ago, the techniques of farming were carried to Scandinavia from the Near East as part of a continuous movement of people, goods, and ideas. Many people of the north abandoned their nomadic way of life and settled into permanent communities to grow grain and raise livestock.

Other imported technologies that affected life in Scandinavia were concerned with metal working. The art of making jewellery and weapons of bronze reached the north about 1500 B.C., about the time Tutankhamen ruled Egypt. The techniques of smelting iron and of hammering it into tools were introduced in the fourth century B.C., the period when the Greeks dominated the eastern Mediterranean and built the Parthenon.

Without historical records, it is difficult to know exactly how or why a new technology or object spread from place to place. Was the technique carried by a group either invading or coming to settle in an area? Did the change come about through trade or peaceful contact among individuals? We will probably never know.

What we do know, however, is that by the time iron tools and weapons were made in Scandinavia, various ethnic groups were clearly identifiable; and the ancestors of the Vikings – the forefathers of the modern Danes, Norwegians, Swedes, and Icelanders – can be traced.

The Roman Iron Age
0 – 400 A.D.

In the two centuries before the birth of Christ, the Romans became the dominant power in the Mediterranean. By the middle of the first century A.D. their Empire included all the lands around the Black Sea and the Mediterranean, as well as Europe west of the Rhine River, and the southern part of Britain.

Although the Romans could not conquer the Germanic tribes of the Rhine, the tribespeople were attracted by the wealth of the Empire. Not surprisingly, conflicts arose with some regularity. Successive emperors attempted to lure the Germanic tribes into the Roman economic sphere. The Romans sent costly gifts to the tribal chiefs, encouraged trade across the frontier, and hired Germanic soldiers to serve as auxiliary troops in the Roman army. In the third and fourth centuries A.D., certain Germanic tribes were allowed to settle just inside the Empire in return for defending a section of the frontier.

Europe at the end of the fourth century, just before the fall of the Roman Empire.

Scandinavian brooch, based on Roman prototypes.
Fourth century

As a result of the interaction between the two peoples, merchants and returning soldiers brought Roman goods into Scandinavia in such quantities that, although Scandinavia was never part of the Empire, the first four centuries A.D. are called the Roman Iron Age.

Much of the imported wealth was in the form of gold and silver coins – more than five thousand Roman coins have been found on the island of Gotland alone – but Roman jewellery, pottery, and vessels of glass, bronze, and silver have also been found. Many of the vessels are cups and strainers used to prepare and serve another import, wine.

Only the wealthiest Scandinavians could afford imported Roman luxuries, but craftsmen created objects imitating Roman fashions for their less prosperous clients. Various types of jewellery, particularly brooches and buckles, were made to Roman models, and pendants imitating Roman coins were also popular.

One of the most interesting imports into the Germanic world was writing. Through trade and travel the Germanic tribes became aware of the Latin and Greek alphabets used within the Roman Empire. They borrowed this concept of written letters and created their own system of writing. The alphabet they developed was made up of twenty-four letters known as runes.

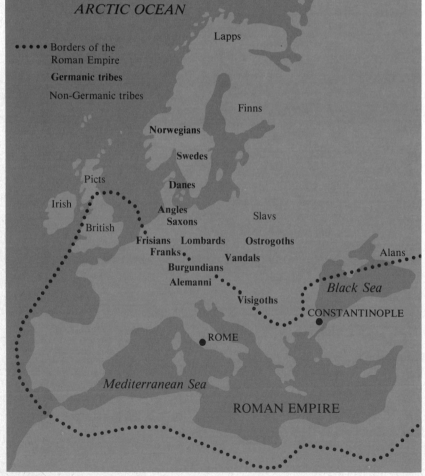

ARCTIC OCEAN

Lapps

• • • • Borders of the
Roman Empire

Germanic tribes

Non-Germanic tribes

Finns

Norwegians

Swedes

Picts

Irish

Danes

British

Angles
Saxons

Slavs

Frisians **Lombards** **Ostrogoths**
Franks **Vandals** Alans
Burgundians
Alemanni *Black Sea*
Visigoths CONSTANTINOPLE

ROME

Mediterranean Sea

ROMAN EMPIRE

Runic alphabets. The top line shows the early Germanic *futhark* of twenty-four characters. The lower line shows the sixteen-letter *futhark* used by the Vikings.

Eleventh-century inscription on a boulder in Uppland, Sweden commemorating a man who died in Russia and was buried at Novgorod.

Some of the runes were adapted from Greek or Roman characters; others were totally new. The runic alphabet or *futhark*, as it is called after the names of its first six characters, was used by many Germanic peoples until the Middle Ages. In some rural areas of Scandinavia, it was used until the nineteenth century, so scholars have been able to trace the development from the common Germanic tongue of modern Germanic languages: German, Dutch, Flemish, Danish, Swedish, Norwegian, Icelandic, and English. The angular runes were well suited for carving in wood and stone, and most surviving runic inscriptions are found on gravestones. However, like any written language, runes were used for many purposes: business letters, statements of ownership ("Ranvaig owns this box"), memorial inscriptions, ad-

vertising ("Thorfast made a good comb"), curses, and, of course, graffiti. In the ninth, tenth, and eleventh centuries, Vikings using the later sixteen-letter version of the futhark left the Scandinavian equivalent of "Kilroy was here" scrawled on stones from Greenland to Istanbul.

The Migration Period
400 A.D. – 550 A.D.

So many European and Asiatic tribes were on the move between 400 and 550 that the period is known as the Migration Period. There were a number of reasons for the migrations. At the end of the fourth century, the Roman Empire began to disintegrate. Germanic tribes swept across the old borders into areas that had been under Roman control for four hundred years. The Visigoths forced their way across the frontier to escape from the Huns, a nomadic tribe from the Russian steppes. Other groups crossed the frontier to take political and economic control of vulnerable portions of the old Empire. The Franks, a Germanic tribe living near the mouth of the Rhine, gradually took over much of present-day Germany and France, the land that took their name.

Further north, over-population, famine, soil depletion, or cattle disease may have driven the Germanic tribes of Scandinavia and Germany to seek greener pastures abroad. Angles and Jutes from Denmark joined with Saxons from

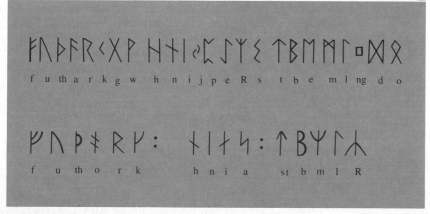

f u t h a r k g w   h n i j p e R s   t b e   m l ng d o

f u t h o r k   h n i a   st b m l R

The fortress of Eketorp on the island of Gotland.

Hoard of gold armrings found in a bog on the island of Öland.
Third century

northern Germany to conquer Britain. They forced the native Celtic population into the mountains of Wales, and the Celtic island of Britain was transformed into the Germanic country of *Angle-land* or England.

During the times of trouble in the Empire there was also a period of unrest within Scandinavia. Many settlements in the west of Denmark were deserted, and archaeologists have excavated the remains of two farms on the island of Bornholm that were burned to the ground. The Scandinavians built many fortresses, generally simple structures of earth and stone, just large enough to protect farm families and their livestock. But the inhabitants of the island of Öland built a series of elaborate fortresses that remained in use for several hundred years. The most famous of these is Eketorp. The fort has

a circular stone rampart 80 m (263 ft.) in diameter and about 6 m (19 ft.) high. Inside, there are about twenty buildings arranged like the spokes of a wheel around a central courtyard.

Yet the fortresses and the unsettled nature of the Migration Period belie the times, for this was literally a "golden age" in Scandinavian history. Hundreds of hoards of gold jewellery and coins have been found, the largest containing more than 12 k (26 lbs.) of gold. Neckrings weighing more than a kilo (two pounds) each have also been discovered. The gold generally entered Scandinavia in the form of coins from the Mediterranean, but

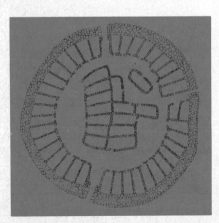

it was quickly converted into armrings, neckrings, gold-plated sword hilts, and bracteates, circular pendants of gold foil embossed with designs imitating the motifs on Roman coins.

Three types of gold hoards have been discovered. The first is literally "buried treasure," valuables temporarily buried to keep them safe during troubled times. However, other hoards were meant to stay in the ground forever. During the Roman Iron Age and the Migration Period, gold, weapons, jewellery, clothing, household and farming implements, ships, animals, and people were thrown into peat bogs. The custom was particularly widespread in Denmark, and the objects were probably an offering to the gods for the fertility of the crops or victory in battle.

Gold was also buried in graves. Before the adoption of Christianity in the tenth and eleventh centuries, it was customary to place objects in the grave for the deceased to enjoy in the afterlife. Often the body and burial objects were cremated before being placed in the grave. Nonetheless, the surviving burned fragments often give archaeologists enough information to determine the number and quality

Gilt-bronze brooch. Similar brooches are found in many places settled by Germanic tribespeople during the Migration Period. Sixth century

Fragments of brooch moulds used by craftsmen at Helgö.

The Merovingian Period

550 A.D. – 800 A.D.

of the grave goods. Local customs varied, but the buried goods generally reflected the dead person's status and wealth. A poor person might be buried in his clothes with a simple knife or cloak pin; but the graves of the rich often contained everything necessary for a comfortable afterlife: complete sets of weapons, jewellery, household equipment, cattle, dogs, horses, wagons, ships, and, in a few instances, a slave or concubine.

Beginning in the sixth century, a series of graves in Scandinavia were created that are so elaborate they must be the graves of chieftains. Many are under mounds so large that only a chieftain would have commanded the manpower needed to build them. One such mound, at Raknehaugen, near Oslo, Norway, is 15 m (50 ft.) high and 95 m (312 ft.) in diameter. Constructed with more than 80,000 m^3 (200,000 cu. ft.) of earth and 125,000 logs, it probably took five hundred men an entire summer to build.

Three similar mounds were built at Gamla Uppsala, north of Stockholm, Sweden. The bodies and buried goods had been burned on a pyre before the mounds were raised, but the fragments remaining indicate that the dead had been lavishly supplied with weapons, jewellery, glass vessels, and gold-worked textiles. Legend identifies the bodies as Aun, Egil, and Adils, early kings of the *Svear*, the people who gave their name to Sweden.

Near the grave mounds at Gamla Uppsala is the site of Helgö. The earliest known Scandinavian centre of trade and manufacturing, Helgö may have contributed to the wealth of the chieftains buried at Gamla Uppsala. During the fifth, sixth, and seventh centuries, Helgö was a focal point for Swedish industry. Merchants brought goods to Helgö from all over Europe and the Near East. A small, bronze statue of the Buddha found at the site indicates that some merchants may have gone as far as India. Craftsmen of Helgö practised iron-working, bronze-smithing, bone and antler working, and goldsmithing. Products that may have originated in the Helgö workshops have been found throughout central Sweden.

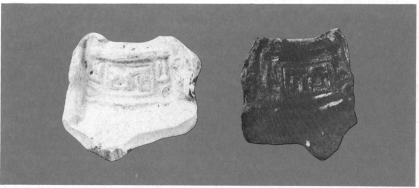

Sword hilt inlaid with cloisonné garnets,
from a grave on Gotland.
Seventh century

Gilt-bronze strap mounts from Gotland,
decorated with stylized animal motifs.
Seventh century

Europe in the eighth century, during the
reign of Charlemagne.

Craftsmen from Helgö may well
have created the spectacular objects found in the grave mounds
at nearby Vendel and Valsgärde.
These cemeteries seem to have
been the burial places of local
chieftains. There is one magnifi-
cently equipped burial site for each
generation, from about 600 A.D. to
1000 A.D. The dead were placed in
ships with their weapons, riding
equipment, and cooking utensils.

Horses and dogs were placed in the
graves, as well as livestock such as
sheep and oxen.

The eighth century was one of
relative peace and prosperity
throughout Europe: the Carolin-
gian Franks ruled most of France
and Germany, their empire reaching its zenith under Charlemagne
during the latter part of the eighth
century. In England, various
Anglo-Saxon kingdoms had come

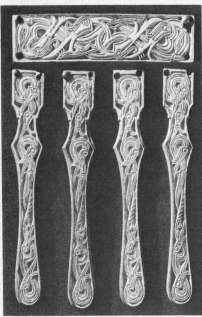

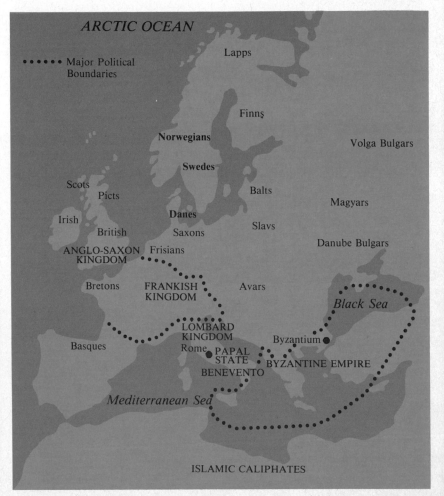

ARCTIC OCEAN

• • • • • Major Political
Boundaries

Lapps

Finns

Norwegians

Swedes

Volga Bulgars

Scots

Picts

Balts

Magyars

Irish

Danes

Slavs

British

Saxons

Danube Bulgars

ANGLO-SAXON   Frisians
KINGDOM

Bretons   FRANKISH   Avars
            KINGDOM

Black Sea

LOMBARD
KINGDOM

Byzantium •

Basques   Rome • PAPAL
                       STATE • BYZANTINE EMPIRE
                 BENEVENTO

Mediterranean Sea

ISLAMIC CALIPHATES

Hoard of silver armrings from Gotland. Armrings like these were made from melted coins and represented a portable bank account.
Tenth century

to an uneasy peace and were prospering. In the East, the Byzantine Empire succeeded the Eastern Roman Empire. The Islamic kingdoms had been expanding rapidly since the middle of the sixth century, and their caliphs vied with the Byzantine emperors for control of the eastern Mediterranean and North Africa.

The conversion of Europe to Christianity was almost complete, and the Church was a great patron of the arts and of commerce. But Christianity was not the only factor uniting Europe: flourishing trade gave European culture another common factor. A pagan nobleman buried at Sutton Hoo in England had objects from England, Ireland, Sweden, Egypt, and Byzantium placed in his grave.

However, trade and prosperity brought unforeseen consequences. As the merchants prospered, so did the Viking pirates who preyed upon them.

The Age of the Vikings
800 A.D. – 1050 A.D.

The word "Viking" means "pirate," and was originally applied to those men who made a living by warfare and plundering, men who went "a-viking." The term was used to describe all the Scandinavians of the ninth to twelfth centuries only much later.

Between the years 790 and 850, shiploads of men terrorized the coasts of Europe, attacking isolated monasteries and undefended towns, wherever there was a reasonable chance of taking loot without undue risk. The pirates arrived suddenly from the sea and had no respect for Christian churches and monasteries. Such blasphemy shocked their victims. The annals of the time, mostly recorded by monks, were the basis for the Vikings' bloodthirsty reputation for the next thousand years.

In the middle of the ninth century, the raids began to change. Individual ships no longer attacked on a hit-and-run basis. Instead, fleets of Viking ships began to appear off the coasts of Germany, France, and the British Isles. The leaders of these expeditions were men who were more interested in carving out personal kingdoms than in booty.

The rulers of England and France paid huge sums of gold and silver as *danegeld* – "Dane's money" – to be left in peace; but the wealth only went to pay the troops, and the attacks continued. In 875, the Viking leader Halfdan conquered the Anglo-Saxon kingdom of Northumbria, in northern England. He divided the land among his followers, and established his seat at York. The Vikings were prevented from overrunning all of England by the young king of Wessex, now known as "Alfred the Great," who rallied the English. In 886, Alfred made a treaty with the Viking leader Guthrum, whereby the Viking lands were limited to the eastern part of England north of the Thames.

The Vikings also threatened the stability of the Frankish kingdoms. After Charlemagne's death in 814, his kingdom was divided among his sons, who were too busy squabbling among themselves to resist the Vikings effectively. It wasn't until 911 that King Charles the Simple granted what is now Normandy in northwestern France to the Viking leader Rollo, in the hope that Rollo would defend the coasts of France from further attacks.

However, even during the periods of greatest Viking aggression, not all Scandinavians were warriors or pirates. In the centuries prior to the Viking Period, there had been a gradual expansion of settlement within Scandinavia up into the mountains and northwards towards the Arctic Circle. By the ninth century, there was little usable land left, and people began to look overseas for new areas to settle. The Danes emigrated to the north and east of England, to land they acquired from the English. The Norwegians settled on islands in the North Atlantic, and on islands off the north and west coasts of Scotland.

From these islands, Viking ships were quick to make their way down the west coast of Scotland to Ireland, where they established the trading posts that developed into the modern towns of Dublin, Limerick, Waterford, Wexford, and Cork. In fact, nearly all the major towns of modern Ireland were founded by the Vikings.

The Faroes and Iceland were virtually uninhabited until the Norse settled there, although Irish monks may have lived there for a short time. From Iceland, Norse settlers moved on to Greenland, where they established two settlements that survived for more than four hundred years. These Norse inhabitants of Greenland were the first Europeans to settle in the New World.

While the Danes and Norwegians lived in Western Europe, the Swedes were busy exploiting the riches of the east. Swedish merchants travelled down the rivers of Russia to Byzantium, where they traded furs, amber, and slaves for the silver, silks, and spices of the Orient. They brought back silver in the form of Arabic coins, which were either melted down for jewellery or cut up into small pieces to buy various goods. The face value of the coins meant nothing to the Vikings; only the weight of silver they contained was important. The silver content was determined by weight using a balance. Small bronze balances and weights have been found in graves that, one assumes, belong to Viking merchants.

The settling of new lands and trading with old ones was paralleled by a dramatic expansion of commerce, which led to the establishment of new towns as trade and industrial centres. The Swedish merchants and craftsmen of Helgö moved to the nearby island of Björkö; there,

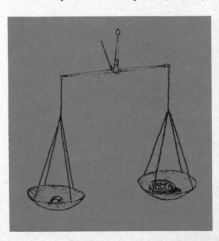

Birka was the most important town in Viking-Period Sweden. More than three thousand graves have been excavated from the cemeteries surrounding Birka.

about the year 800, they founded the town of Birka. Birka was the first true town in Scandinavia, in that its economy depended mainly on trade and industry rather than on agriculture, as had been the case at Helgö. Ribe and Hedeby in Denmark were also founded about the year 800. Hedeby became one of the most important towns in Viking-age Scandinavia; like Birka it was a fortified town, protected by encircling walls and a fortress.

Located at the base of the Jutland peninsula, Hedeby was perfectly situated to command both the north-south traffic in and out of Denmark and the portage route across the neck of Jutland. This portage enabled merchants to avoid the long and sometimes hazardous voyage around the tip of the Jutland peninsula. The passage was so important that it was defended by a wall, known as the *Danevirke*. By the end of the Viking Period, the Danevirke stretched right across the country, and it formed Denmark's southern border until the middle of the nineteenth century. (There does not seem to have been a site in Norway comparable to Birka or Hedeby, although there was an important trading and manufacturing site at Kaupang, south of the modern city of Oslo.)

Two interrelated movements characterize the later Viking Period in Scandinavia: the unification of Norway, Sweden, and Denmark under centralized monarchies, and the conversion of the people to Christianity. The religious conversion was a relatively peaceful and gradual affair. Scandinavians living abroad in Christian France, England, and Ireland rapidly adopted the religion of their new countries, and there were frequent Christian missions to Scandinavia from Germany. The success of the proselytizing movement was due in part to the kings of Scandinavia, who became champions of the Church.

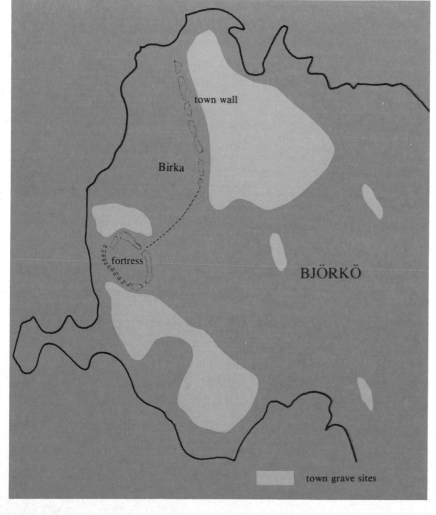

town wall

Birka

fortress

BJÖRKÖ

town grave sites

Rune stone erected at Jelling, Denmark by King Harald Bluetooth in the tenth century. The motif of the great beast in combat with a serpent is a popular one in Viking-Period art.

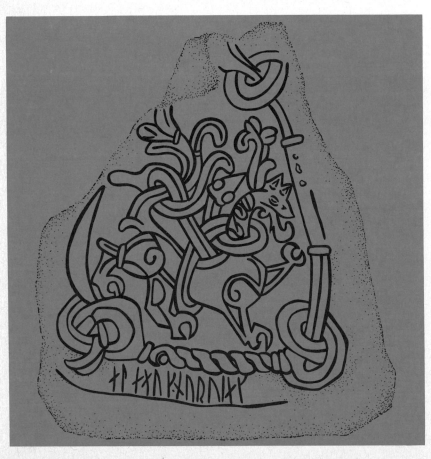

The most famous of the early Christian kings was Harald Bluetooth of Denmark. He erected a monument at Jelling that reads, "Harald had this monument built in memory of Gorm his father and Thyri his mother; that Harald who won all of Denmark and Norway and made the Danes Christian." Unfortunately, the costs of unification were high, and in the beginning of the eleventh century, Harald's son Swein Forkbeard was compelled to attack England to replenish the royal coffers. He conquered England in 1016 and, on his death, his son Canute ruled an empire that encompassed almost all the lands surrounding the North Sea. The empire did not last beyond Canute's lifetime, as his sons were unable to keep it intact. However, it marks the emergence of the Christian kingdoms of Scandinavia into European politics: by the end of the eleventh century, the Viking Age was at a close, and the kingdoms of Norway, Sweden, and Denmark could be counted among the nations of Europe.

Daily Life in Scandinavia

Ornamental rein guide. Decorative pieces like this kept the reins from tangling in the rest of the harness when a horse was pulling a wagon or sleigh.
Ninth or tenth century

Ice skates made from animals' leg bones. Skates like these were used for travelling on frozen lakes and rivers in the winter.
Ninth or tenth century

Although we tend to think of the Vikings as warriors and pirates, most of them spent peaceful lives on farms scattered throughout Scandinavia. Agriculture, not warfare, formed the basis of the Viking economy.

Rural economies varied according to the local environment and resources. In the fertile regions of Denmark and southern Sweden, and on various islands in the Baltic, farmers grew cereal crops such as barley, wheat, and rye; they also raised some livestock. Further to the north, sheep and cattle were the mainstay, as the weather was too cool and the summers too short for grain to grow properly. In the mountainous regions of Norway, sheep and cattle were taken to summer pastures high in the mountains; the little pockets of farmland nestled on the coast were used to grow grains, vegetables, and the hay needed to feed the animals during the winter.

Hunting and fishing were important in almost all areas: birds, fish, and wild animals provided not only food, but also raw materials and goods for export. Walrus was hunted for its ivory tusks and for

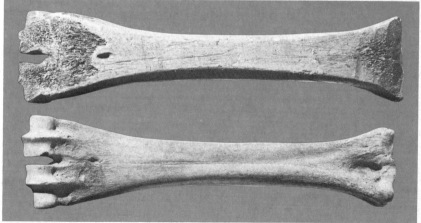

Reconstruction of a Migration-Period farmhouse.

Reconstruction of a Viking-Period house.

The Viking Household

A typical farm consisted of several buildings surrounded by fences or stone walls. During the Migration Period, the main building was often a long, rectangular house; the hearth and living quarters were at one end, and stalls for livestock were at the other. A settlement excavated at Vallhagar, on the island of Gotland, included several houses of this type. In all, twenty-four buildings belonging to five or six separate farms were found at the site. Each house had limestone walls and a double row of posts to support the roof, which was probably thatched or covered with turf. Some of the excavated houses had been destroyed by fire. Samples of burned grain show that the farmers at Vallhagar raised barley, wheat, and rye; animal bones indicate that they kept sheep, cattle, pigs, and horses. The bones of a cat that had been trapped by the fire were found in one of the houses.

Viking-Period farmhouses were very similar to those of the Migration Period, except that the animals were housed in their own building. The typical house of the Viking Period was a rectangular building with a central hearth. Low platforms were built along the long walls for sitting and sleeping.

Some houses had separate rooms at one or both ends, which were probably used as storerooms. Extra rooms for storage or accommodation were added as they were needed.

Construction methods varied from place to place according to what building materials were available. In the forested regions of Norway and Sweden, houses were built of wood. Viking colonists living on the sparsely treed islands in the North Atlantic built their houses of stone and turf. The houses excavated at Hedeby and other Viking towns are similar to farmhouses but not as solidly built. The Hedeby buildings were made of wooden planks or of wattle and daub. Wattles are panels of woven branches, usually willow. They are inserted in a wooden framework and then plastered with daub, a mixture of mud, straw, and cattle dung. This method of construction is not as flimsy as it might sound. The black and white Tudor cottages usually associated with Shakespeare were built in this manner, and many of them are still standing four hundred years later.

its hide, which made excellent ships' rope. Beaver and marten furs were very valuable, and were often exported to distant areas. The antlers of red and roe deer were used to make combs, knife handles, buttons, and other objects.

Bronze key, worn by the housewife almost as a badge of office.
Eighth century

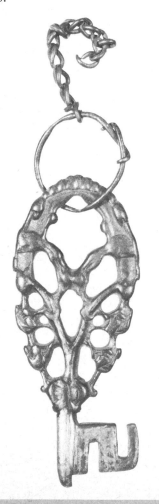

The atmosphere within a Viking house would have been rather pungent. There were no windows or chimney; smoke from the fireplace made its way out through openings in the peak of the roof or gable ends.

Very little is known about the way the houses were furnished. Simple benches and tables were used, although none survives. Spare clothing and valuables were kept in wooden chests, which were often secured with iron padlocks. The keys to these chests were worn by the woman in charge of the household as a badge of office. We know that some people had beds – a beautifully carved wooden bedstead was included among the grave goods of a woman buried in a Viking ship at Oseberg, Norway – but a bed must have been a great luxury. Ordinary people wrapped themselves in cloaks and furs, and slept on the platforms or on the floor as close to the fire as they could safely get. Warmth, not privacy, was prized.

On the farm, men were responsible for the heavy agricultural work, for hunting and fishing, and for building the houses and keeping them in good repair. The women were responsible for the care of the children, providing clothing for the family, and preparing the wide variety of foods that were available according to the region and the time of year. Beef, pork, mutton, goat, and horse were all eaten, as was the meat of such wild animals as deer, elk, boar, and bear. Farms raised chickens and geese, and in the Atlantic regions sea birds were hunted for their eggs. Cattle, sheep, and goats were also kept for milk, butter, and cheese. Those

animals that could not be wintered over or were too weak to withstand the cold were slaughtered in the autumn. Their flesh was preserved by salting or by pickling in brine or whey. Fish was another important source of protein, and the meat of seals and whales was enjoyed in certain areas.

Food was cooked in cauldrons made of iron or soapstone. These were held over the fire hanging from either an iron tripod or a chain from the rafters. Meat was boiled or roasted on a spit over an open fire. Meat and fish were also roasted in pits or ovens pre-heated with red-hot stones.

Fruits and vegetables were eaten in season. Peas, cabbage, onions, and such seasonings as garlic, horseradish, mustard, and cumin were grown on the farms, and the seeds of apples, plums, cherries, and a host of wild berries have been found at Hedeby.

Bread was made from barley, rye, wheat, or oats. The grain was ground in a rotary quern made of two circular stones, one on top of the other. The top stone had a hole in the middle into which the grain was poured. When the stone was turned, the grain was crushed between the stones and the flour trickled out the sides. These querns tended to crumble slightly as the grain was ground, and the grit incorporated into the flour wore down the peoples' teeth noticeably.

Wine was imported, and mead was made from honey; but the favourite drink was undoubtedly beer. It was the housewife's responsibility to see that her guests did not go thirsty during the feasts and festivals that sometimes lasted for several days.

Clothing and Adornments

Women were also kept busy spinning and weaving wool and linen cloth needed for clothing, ships' sails, tents, and a host of other purposes. The linen was made from stems of the flax plant that had been soaked and reduced to a fibrous mass. These fibres were handled in much the same way as was raw wool. The wool or flax was first combed so that all the fibres lay in the same direction. The material was then placed on a distaff, a notched stick usually held in the crook of the left arm. Individual strands were attached to a spindle, a short stick with a clay or stone weight, known as a spindle whorl, at the bottom. The spindle was dropped with a twist and, as it fell, the wool or flax was drawn out and spun into a thread.

After spinning, the thread would be dyed. Dyes were extracted from a variety of plants and minerals; several shades of brown, black, red, yellow, green, and blue could be obtained.

Fabric was woven on an upright loom that leaned against the wall of the house. Threads attached to a horizontal beam at the top of the

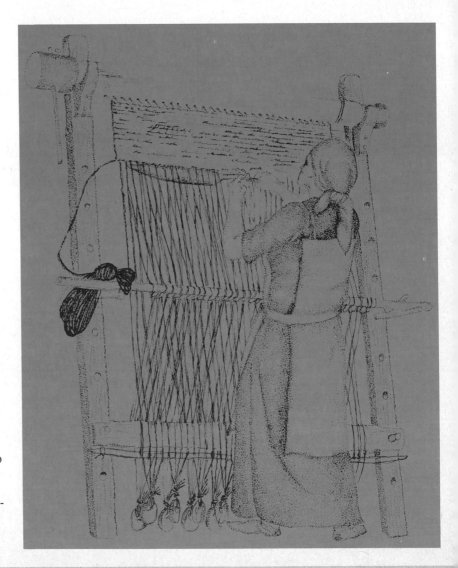

Viking-Period costumes. The woman is spinning thread with a spindle and distaff.

Jewellery from the grave of a Viking woman. The oval brooches would have fastened the shoulder straps of her pinafore, while the small, rectangular brooch secured her shawl.
Ninth or tenth century

loom had clay or stone weights attached to their lower ends to keep them taut. Every second thread was held forward by a shed rod; the remaining threads were connected to a heddle bar. When the bar was pulled toward the weaver, the attached threads were pulled between and in front of the threads in the shed rod. This allowed the horizontal threads to be woven without being twined over and under each individual vertical thread.

The woven fabric was made into clothing. Men's clothing changed little from the beginning of the Roman Iron Age until the end of the Viking Period. The well-dressed Scandinavian man wore woollen trousers and a shirt or tunic made of wool or linen. The trousers were usually long and fairly close fitting. However, during the Viking Period, baggy knee-length trousers enjoyed a temporary vogue, perhaps as the result of trade with the Near East. A woollen cloak was held by a brooch on the right shoulder, leaving the sword arm free. Leather shoes, a belt and, perhaps, a hat completed the ensemble.

Women wore long, woollen dresses, with cloaks in cold or wet weather. During the Viking Period, women's costumes became quite elaborate. A long dress of fine wool or linen was worn under a sort of pinafore, held in place by straps or loops secured by a brooch on either shoulder. Typical

brooches were gilded bronze, covered with intricate animal motifs. Beads were worn around the neck or fastened like garlands between the brooches. The brooches served in place of pockets: combs, keys, needles, and tweezers were often hung from them. A third brooch fastened the shawl or cloak in the middle of the chest, leaving the arms free. This brooch was usually a different shape and style from those securing the pinafore, and was often imported.

Both men and women adorned themselves with jewellery of gold, silver, and bronze. Much of the jewellery was practical, serving the function of modern zippers, buttons, and snaps. However, some jewellery was purely ornamental, and served simply to proclaim the wealth and taste of the wearer.

Animal-head brooch from Gotland. Women on Gotland preferred brooches like this to the oval brooches fashionable throughout the rest of the Viking world.
Ninth century

Viking sword. The pommel and guards are inlaid with silver and copper.
Ninth century

Spearhead decorated with silver inlay.
Tenth century

Battle axe. Axes of this type were primarily weapons, but they could also be used for chopping wood.
Ninth or tenth century

Weapons were also an indication of status. All free men were entitled to carry weapons, but the type and number of the weapons and the amount of ornamentation on them varied according to an individual's wealth and prestige. Spears, knives, and axes were the most common weapons, and were used for hunting and woodworking as well as warfare. Wealthier men carried swords, often with elaborately ornamented hilts. Their wooden shields were covered with leather, a central iron boss protecting the fist holding the shield.

Migration-Period shields often held gilded bronze studs decorated with fantastic animal motifs. Only the wealthiest freemen could afford coats of mail or helmets. Contrary to popular belief, Scandinavian helmets did not have horns; they were smoothly rounded or conical to deflect a sword or axe. The horns were an impractical and romantic invention of the nineteenth century; they would have caught rather than deflected the enemy blade, and a savage blow would have broken the wearer's neck.

The importance of personal cleanliness in Scandinavian society seems to depend on one's point of view. An Arab writer of the tenth century described the Vikings he met in Russia as the "filthiest of God's creatures." But an Englishman writing at about the same time complained that the Scandinavians in his country were so meticulous about bathing and combing their hair that they "disturbed the chastity" of the local beauties.

Two men playing a board game. The image comes from a Swedish rune stone. Note the drinking horn in the hand of the man on the right.

Comb made of antler. Combs like this are frequently found in graves and on settlement sites.
Tenth century

Bone playing pieces for a board game similar to checkers.
Ninth or tenth century

Leisure Pastimes

Viking life was not all work, and leisure time was spent in games and storytelling. A wide variety of games of skill and chance were enjoyed by both sexes. Playing pieces for a game similar to checkers have been found in many graves, and dice made of walrus ivory have been found on several sites. In Iceland, as in other parts of Scandinavia, storytelling and poetry were held in particularly high regard. Much of this oral literature was written down in the thirteenth century and survives to the present day. The *sagas* are a series of prose narratives loosely based on historical events depicting the lives of the more flamboyant members of society. The *Edda* is a collection of poems dealing with the deeds of legendary heroes and pagan Norse mythology.

The most important Norse gods were Odin, Frey, and Thor. The chief of the gods was Odin, the god of poetry and battle. Men slain in combat supposedly went to him after death, escorted by the fierce warrior maidens known as Valkyries. Frey was the god of fertility. He and his sister Freya watched over crops and livestock, increasing yields and herds. Thor, the thunderer, was particularly popular towards the end of the Viking Period, when many people had converted to Christianity.

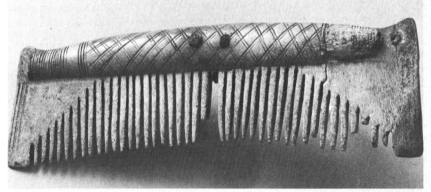

Silver pendant in the shape of Thor's hammer.
Eleventh century

Silver crucifix.
Tenth century

Amulets in the shape of his hammer, Mjolnir, were often worn in the way the Christians wore small crucifixes. The two faiths were not necessarily hostile to each other, and many people accepted elements of both. One Christian settler in Iceland named his farm *Kristnes*, "Christ's point," but invoked Thor before setting out on a sea voyage. The pagan Vikings were fairly tolerant about religious matters, perhaps because religion did not play the central role in daily life that Christianity did in later centuries.

Craft and Industry

Prior to the Viking Period, Scandinavian craftsmen were not concentrated in towns. Many were farmers who also produced goods. Iron smelting and blacksmithing in particular supplemented farm incomes, especially in areas of Sweden where iron ore was plentiful and good farmland at a premium. Jewellers and weapon smiths probably attended the chieftains, either as paid craftsmen or as slaves. Moreover, itinerant craftsmen set up temporary workshops on farms and at seasonal markets, staying as long as business lasted.

About 800 A.D., craftsmen began to congregate in towns like Birka and Hedeby. Such centres were springing up all over Scandinavia as a result of the dramatic expansion of trade during the Viking Period. In towns, craftsmen could contact merchants and farmers bringing in raw materials from rural Scandinavia and abroad. They also had access to a steady market for their wares: individual customers lived in the towns, as did merchants who would resell the goods elsewhere. Excavations at Birka and Hedeby as well as in the Viking levels of Dublin and York have shown that a wide variety of trades were carried on in Viking towns: iron working, weapon smithing, jewellery making, bead making, carpentry, boat building, bone and antler carving, stone carving, tanning, and shoe-making. Many techniques were not that different from those used by craftsmen today.

Iron Working

Iron ore was found in peat bogs throughout much of Scandinavia. This bog-ore, as it is called, was easy to collect. The ore was first dug from the bog and allowed to dry. Then it was ground or pounded into small pieces, and the inferior ore was weeded out. The ore was then converted into metallic iron. The conversion process, known as smelting, ideally took place close to the source of the ore, but only if there was also a sufficient supply of timber nearby to make the charcoal for stoking the smelting furnace.

The furnace was usually constructed by digging a pit about 1 m (3 ft.) in diameter and 0.5 m (18 in.) deep. Over the pit, a chimney of clay was built on a framework of woven willow branches. The chimney was filled with charcoal and the furnace was heated to 1100°C – 1150°C (2000°F – 2100°F). Bellows forced air through the furnace and sped the heating process, but it still took about twenty-four hours to bring it up to temperature. When the furnace was hot, the iron ore was poured in and the temperature maintained until the ore was converted into metallic iron. The chemical transformation of ore to iron is a relatively simple one.

Oxygen in the iron ore combines with the carbon monoxide given off by the burning charcoal; this produces free iron and carbon dioxide. The impurities in the ore were converted by the heat into a glassy waste product known as slag, which ran into the pit below the chimney.

At the end of the smelting process, which took at least a day, the furnace was allowed to cool. It was then broken down, and the porous iron mass, known as bloom, was removed. The bloom still contained some slag, which had to be removed in order that the iron could be consolidated. This was done by a process known as forging, whereby the bloom was repeatedly heated until soft, and hammered until all the slag was removed. The iron never became hot enough to melt; the technique of melting iron and pouring it into moulds to produce objects by casting was not known in Europe until several centuries after the Viking Period.

The iron was forged into rods, bars, or roughly shaped tools. It was then ready to be sold to the blacksmiths, weapon smiths, ship builders, and carpenters, who used iron tools and nails in their work.

Iron working was so important that most farms were equipped to make and repair iron objects. However, iron production and the manufacture of tools and weapons were also carried out on an industrial basis.

Blacksmith's tools, including hammer, anvil, and tongs.

Iron knife. Knives of this sort were carried by most people to cut food and to perform other small chores.
Ninth or tenth century

Section of a pattern-welded blade, showing the twisted rods at the core and the smooth steel edges.

The Blacksmith

Most iron working was done by the blacksmith, who apparently enjoyed relatively high social status. As smith's tools are frequently found in graves dating from the seventh through eleventh centuries, it would seem that the smith was buried with his tools as a warrior was buried with his weapons – to proclaim his status and occupation.

The blacksmith forged the iron blanks produced by the smelter into a wide variety of tools and artifacts: ploughshares, sickles, and scythes for the farmer; axes, adzes, saws, chisels, drills, and files for the carpenter; spears, arrows, and fish hooks for the hunter; locks and keys, hinges, and nails for the house builder; and cauldrons for the housewife. The iron was first heated in the open fire on the forge. The smith's assistant or apprentice, pumping away at the bellows, ensured that the fire burned brightly. When the iron reached the right temperature, which was gauged by its colour, it was removed from the forge with a pair of tongs, placed on a stone or iron anvil, and hammered into shape.

Large items, such as cauldrons, were made from thin sheets of iron. These were hammered out and then joined with rivets. Separate pieces of iron could also be welded together. This technique, which was fundamental in making weapons, involved hammering two pieces of iron together until they fused.

The Weapon Smith

The most elaborate products of the smith's forge were weapons, and few smiths mastered the techniques involved in creating a fine sword or spearhead. The amount of carbon in iron is critical in weapon-making. Iron with less than 0.3% carbon is very soft and can be easily bent – the purer the iron, the softer it is. (This kind of iron is used today for ornamental railings and the like.) When the carbon content exceeds 0.3%, we have

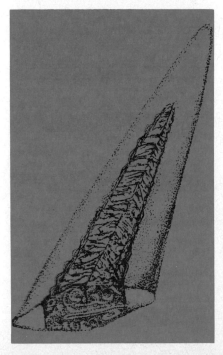

The Jeweller

what we call steel. It is much harder and will keep a sharp edge, but it is rather brittle. Therefore, the finest swords and spears were not hammered out of a single rod of iron. Rather, the smith twisted and welded together several thin rods of different grades of low- and high-carbon iron; the resulting laminated rod was both flexible and resilient. He then welded on an edge of hard steel, and polished and etched the blade with acid. The twisted rods in the core created a flame-like pattern, making the sword as beautiful as it was deadly.

Weapons were usually decorated with inlay or incrustation. Inlay involves cutting a pattern in the surface of the metal and hammering a metal of a different colour into the grooves. Some sword blades from the Viking Period are inlaid with the name of the sword maker. Incrustation is a related technique: the entire surface is incised with fine grooves. Then thin wires or sheets of precious metal are hammered onto the surface, covering it completely. Silver, gold, and copper wires were often used in sequence to create geometric patterns. Some weapons were so ornate that it is difficult to determine where the art of the weapon smith ended and that of the jeweller began.

Most of the raw materials used by the jeweller were imported. Although some gold and silver were mined in Europe, most was imported from the Mediterranean, primarily as coins. The copper and tin used to make bronze were also imported, though the sources of these metals are uncertain.

Gold and silver were the easiest metals to work with. They are both very malleable, and have a low melting temperature; this makes them easy to hammer and

Repoussé gold foil plaque impressed with
the figure of a man.
Seventh century

Detail of a gold collar from Möne, Sweden.
Sixth century

cast. One of the simplest decorative techniques used on gold and silver was that of the punch. Simple armrings were made by hammering out strips of metal into the shape desired, stamping a few dots or lines on them with a punch made of iron, wood, or bone, and then coiling them into a circle. Punches were also used to make bracteates, which were popular from the fifth to the tenth century in Scandinavia. The design of these pendants derived from motifs found on Roman coins. First, the gold was beaten into a thin sheet. It was then struck with a punch that raised the design on the underside of the metal, which became the front of the pendant.

Repoussé was a related technique used for raising designs in thin sheets of gold or silver. The metal was pressed against a matrix of metal, clay, or wood to raise the design from the underside. This gentle technique could be used to transfer designs to very thin sheets of gold foil.

Although repoussé and punching are simple techniques, Scandinavian goldsmiths combined them with other techniques to produce objects of great beauty and complexity. A gold collar found at Mone, Sweden, dating from the sixth century A.D., illustrates many of the techniques used by Scandinavian jewellers. The collar is made of seven hollow tubes of gold. These were created by hammering thin strips of gold around a rod, which was subsequently removed. The tubes were wrapped with fine strands of twisted gold wire, laid in alternate directions to create a herring-bone effect. The wire was made by pulling the gold through successively smaller holes in an iron draw plate; gold wire as fine as 0.5 mm (1/64 in.) in diameter was made by this method. Between the tubes there are small, highly stylized figures of animals made of filigree wire and minute gold beads mounted on small repoussé plaques to heighten the three-dimensional effect.

Gold sword pommel ornamented with garnet cloisonné. There are small, embossed, gold foils behind the garnets to reflect the light.
Sixth century

Crucibles found at Helgö. Crucibles like these were used when melting metal or glass.

Silver pendant in the form of a man's head. Ninth century

Filigree involves nicking wire at regular intervals or squeezing it in a small press to make it look like a string of small beads. The actual gold beads on the collar were made by another process called granulation. Small chips of gold were heated almost to the melting point. As the gold begins to melt, it forms a small sphere before turning completely liquid. If the gold is removed from the heat at that precise instant, it will retain the form of a perfect little sphere of gold. The filigree and granules were attached to the repoussé plaques by fusion. They were heated until their surfaces were slightly molten and would stick together. Fusion demands great skill in controlling the heat: if the gold is not heated sufficiently, the pieces will not bond; if it is heated too much, they will melt.

During the period 400–800, gold jewellery was often inlaid with garnets, opaque stones, and glass paste. The stones were set in cloisons, individual cells with raised walls made of thin metal strips set on edge. The stones were secured with mastic, a resinous gum prepared from the saps of various trees. The whole surface of the piece was then polished flat. Garnets, often cut into intricate shapes, were the most popular stone used in cloisonnée. Gold foil was often placed beneath the stones to reflect the light.

Scandinavian jewellers also made products by casting. Molten bronze, gold, or silver was poured into a mould; when it had cooled, the finished object was removed.

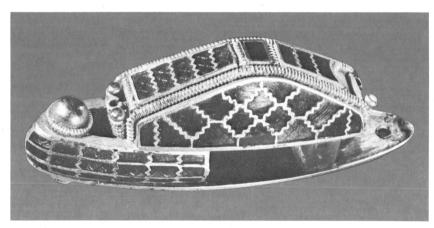

Drum-shaped brooch from Gotland, made of bronze, ornamented with silver, niello, and applied gold foils with filigree and granulation.
Tenth century

The simplest pieces were cast in an open mould of stone, clay, or antler, which could be re-used. More complex pieces were cast in closed moulds. These were made by one of two methods: the lost wax or *cire perdue* method or the split cast method.

The lost wax method of casting was used for delicate items, such as the ninth-century silver pendant in the shape of a man's head found at Aska, Sweden. A wax model of the desired object was made and coated with clay. A small opening was left in the clay so that, when it was baked, the wax would run out. Heated metal was poured into the mould through the opening. After the metal had cooled inside the mould, the mould was broken away and the finished object removed.

Using the split mould method, one surface of a wax or clay model or piece of jewellery was covered with clay, which was allowed to dry. The model was removed, and the mould baked to harden it. A similar mould was made for the other surface, and the two halves of the mould were put together. Liquid metal was then poured into the space between the two halves.

When the metal had cooled, the mould was broken cleanly along the line where the two halves joined. This second technique was used by the jewellers who produced the masses of bronze jewellery worn by men and women on an every-day basis to secure their clothing.

Most jewellery was made of bronze, but it was often gilded to imitate the gold jewellery worn by the wealthy. To do this, the object was covered with a mixture of powdered gold and mercury, a very volatile and unstable metal. When it was heated, the mercury vaporized and left behind a thin film of gold.

In order to create a polychrome effect, jewellers combined the yellow glitter of gold, the white of silver, and a black inlay called *niello*, which was a mixture of copper, silver, and sulphur. A tenth-century brooch from Gotland illustrates this effect, as well as most others known to Norse craftsmen. The brooch is made from gilded cast bronze. The applied side panels and edge are incrusted with silver inlaid with niello. The open fields on the top and sides are filled with small gold repoussé panels ornamented with filigree and granulation. This brooch displays virtually every technique in the jeweller's repertoire, and is a virtuoso performance.

Making a comb from antler.

Bead Making

The art of making glass from sand and potash was unknown in Scandinavia during the Viking Period; but glass was imported in large quantities. Some was in the form of the wine cups and drinking horns used by the wealthy. However, broken glass and coloured glass tiles or *tesserae* taken from old Roman mosaics were also imported for bead making.

In order to make beads, the glass was melted in crucibles and then pulled out into strands like taffy. A length of glass was placed around a tapered iron rod and the ends were joined to make a bead. The process was repeated the length of the rod. When the beads were cool, they were slipped off the tapered end of the rod and were ready for stringing. Beads made of semi-precious stones such as amethyst, carnelian, and rock crystal have been found in graves and sites in Scandinavia. The stones were definitely imported, but it is not certain whether they were made into beads before their importation. We do know, however, that the Scandinavians made beads from amber, which has a lovely, reddish-orange hue and gives off a faint scent of pine when warmed by the heat of the body.

Bone and Antler Working

Bone and antler were to the tenth century very much what plastic is to the twentieth: strong, resilient, versatile, inexpensive, and readily obtainable. Bone was provided by the animals slaughtered for food, and deer shed their antlers each year after the mating season. One of the most important of the wide variety of products from antler was combs. Four or five rectangular plates of antler about 2 cm by 3 cm (1 in. by 1^1/$_2$ in.) were rivetted between two thin rods of the same material. The teeth were then cut with a small saw; the back of the comb might be decorated with incised lines or circles.

Soapstone Carving

Pottery cooking vessels were not widely used in Scandinavia during the Viking Period. Instead, food was cooked in pots made of iron or soapstone, a soft, talc-like stone that can be easily carved with a knife. It is found in out-croppings in various parts of Norway, and was shipped to other parts of Scandinavia. Soapstone was also used for spindle whorls, loom weights, and fishing-line sinkers.

Carpentry

All Viking men had some knowledge of carpentry and iron working. Wood was readily available and was vital for houses, ships, wagons, tool handles, cooking and eating vessels, and barrels for storing grain, milk, beer, pickled fish, and meat. The tools used by Scandinavian carpenters would be familiar to us today, and most of them are still in use. Only the adze, which has been replaced by the power saw, and the spoon auger, which has been superseded by the spiral-shaped drill bit, would be out of place in a modern tool kit.

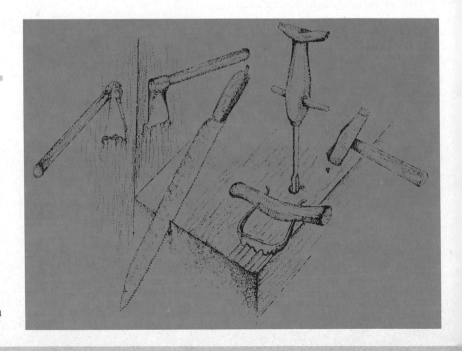

Ships and Shipbuilding

Scandinavians have been building boats of one type or another for more than five thousand years. The earliest boats were dug-out canoes, made by hollowing out large tree trunks. Several of these canoes have survived, the oldest dated to around 3500 B.C.

Ships are common motifs in rock carvings dated to about 1500 B.C. The ships in the carvings look like they are made of animal hides stretched over a wooden framework. The bottom plank appears to extend forwards and upwards, perhaps to protect the skins when the boat was beached.

The oldest surviving boat made of wooden planks was found in a bog at Hjortspring, Denmark. The planks were sewn together with cord, and the seams were caulked with a resin glue. The top and bottom planks were extended front and back, and the boat resembled those in the rock carvings. The planks were lashed to the ribs with strips of hazel wood in a manner characteristic of early Viking shipbuilding. The Hjortspring ship was 12.2 m (40 ft.) long; judging from the number of paddles discovered in the ship, it probably carried a crew of twenty.

In the middle of the second century A.D., the Roman author Tacitus described the ships of the *Suiones* or Swedes. He commented on the fact that the ships had no sails, and that they were pointed at each end so they were always facing the right way. Contemporary ships on the Mediterranean had a blunt stern, which contrasted with the sharply pointed bow, and they were propelled by both sail and oars.

A ship, dating from about 350 A.D., was found in a bog at Nydam, Denmark. It displays features generally associated with Viking ships. The hull is 25 m (75 ft.) long, and is constructed of overlapping horizontal planks nailed together. This type of construction is known as "clinker building." The planks, or "strakes" as they are properly called, are lashed to the internal ribs. The Nydam ship was rowed rather than paddled. The fifteen oarlocks on each side of the ship acted as a fulcrum for the oars and greatly enhanced the speed and manoeuvrability of the ship. The ship has a high bow and stern, and a fixed steering oar at the stern, so it looks somewhat like a typical Viking ship. However, this is where the resemblance ends. The strakes of the Nydam ship are built up from a broad bottom plank, rather than from a strong central spine or keel present on true Viking ships.

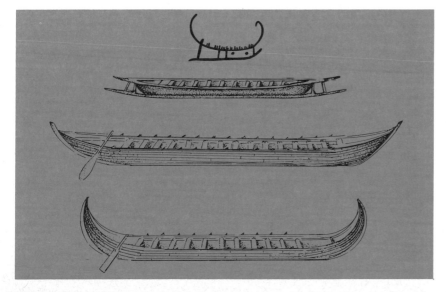

About 700 A.D., a ship was buried at Kvalsund, Norway. It is the first Scandinavian ship found that displays a true keel, and it was capable of carrying a mast and sail, although there is no evidence that it did so. The hull is broader than that of the Nydam ship, even though the Kvalsund ship is more than 3 m (10 ft.) shorter. The oak planks are built up from the keel to form a strong, flexible shell, and the bow and stern rise to graceful points.

The strength of the keel and the ability to carry sails are closely related, for a sturdy keel is absolutely vital to a sailing ship. It not only supports the weight and pressure of the mast, but it keeps the boat from moving sideways when sailed at an angle to the wind, and translates the lateral pressure of the wind on the sails into forward motion. Scandinavian ships were fitted with sails during the eighth century. Contemporary incised and painted stones found on the island of Gotland show ships under sail.

The stones depict a single rectangular sail suspended from a horizontal yard at the top of the mast. A complicated system of interlacing lines covers the surface of the pictured sail. However, as no sails of the time survive, it is not known whether the lines represent the rigging – that is, the ropes used to control the sail – or bands sewn to the body of the sail to reinforce the loosely woven cloth.

The oldest preserved Scandinavian ship with a mast and sail dates from about the year 800 A.D., the dawn of the Viking Period. This is one of the most famous of the surviving Viking ships, and was preserved in a burial mound at Oseberg, Norway. It formed part of the burial goods of a woman whose grave is one of the richest and best preserved in Scandinavia. (In addition to the ship, the grave contained a complete set of household equipment: cooking utensils, food, beds, bedding, clothing and tapestries, a loom, a wagon, three sledges, three horses, thirteen dogs, an ox, and a serving woman. It also contained some of the finest surviving examples of Viking wood carving. The ship, the wagon, and two of the sledges were all richly ornamented with stylized animal motifs.)

The ship is 21.4 m (71 ft. 6 in.) long and 5.1 m (17 ft.) wide. The prow and stern sweep up gracefully and end in spirals 5.0 m (16 ft. 6 in.) above the surface of the

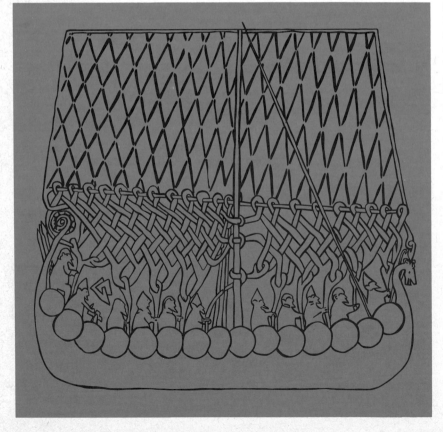

water. The Oseberg ship displays
the structural characteristics of a
true Viking ship: the sides were
built up from the keel in a series
of overlapping strakes to form a
light, flexible shell supported by
transverse ribs, which were added
at a later stage. A heavy beam
known as the "keelson" or "mast
partner" lay on top of the keel to
support the base of the mast and
distribute its weight. The mast was
given added support by a second
beam at deck level. Called the
mast fish because of its shape, this
beam is slotted to allow the mast
to be raised and lowered. In addition to the mast and sails, the Oseberg ship had fifteen pairs of oars,
which passed through oar-ports in
the top strake.

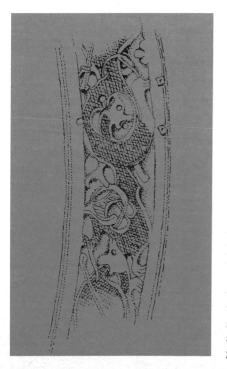

However, for all her grace and
beauty, the Oseberg ship was not a
seaworthy, ocean-going vessel. The
keel was made of two pieces of
rather thin oak, which would have
severely compromised its strength.
The stem and stern posts are also
jointed. The oar-ports are only
about 10 cm (4 in.) above the
water line, so the boat would ship
large quantities of water in even
moderately rough seas. Moreover,
the deck planking was nailed down
in all but a few places, which
would have made bailing difficult.
These factors seem to indicate that
the ship was meant only for relatively sheltered waters in calm
weather. She may have been a
pleasure barge belonging to the
woman buried in her.

Perhaps the most beautiful surviving Viking ship is that found in
a burial mound at Gokstad, not
far from Oseberg, Norway. The
burial mound, like the burial
mound at Oseberg, was made of
blue clay. This totally sealed out
the air and prevented the wood
from decomposing. (Both the Gok
stad and Oseberg ships can be seen
today in the Viking Ship Museum
outside Oslo.)

The Gokstad ship is 23.0 m (76 ft.)
long and 5.2 m (17 ft.) at the
widest point. Her keel was carved
from a single oak. It was shaped
with axe and adze to be thickest at
the middle, where it would have to
support the weight of the mast,
and tapered at each end to help it
glide through the water. The sides

of the keel were notched so that
the strakes would lie smoothly
against it. The sides of the ship
were built up from sixteen oak
strakes on either side. The logs for
the strakes were split radially into
halves, quarters, eighths, and,
finally, thirty-seconds; such planks
are very strong, because the grain
of the wood is not cut. The planks
were then individually shaped to
produce the beautiful swelling
curves of the hull. Cleats were left
on the insides of the strakes for
attaching the ribs. A groove chis-
eled along the lower edge of each
strake was packed with tarred wool
when the ship was assembled,
making the joints waterproof. The
strakes were fastened together with
iron rivets, which were passed
from the inside of the ship and
hammered or "clenched" down
over a small iron plate on the
outside.

The nineteen ribs were inserted at
intervals of about 1 m (3 ft.) after
the first ten strakes had been
fitted. They were carved from
naturally curved timbers to fit the
interior of the hull. Willow roots
or *whithies* were used to tie the
ribs to the cleats that projected
from the inner surfaces of the
strakes. After the ribs were secure,
the builders lowered in place the
timber keelson, so massive that it
spanned four ribs. Then horizontal
crossbeams were inserted to help
hold the sides of the ship apart,
and to give it strength when it
heeled over under the pressure of
the wind in the sail. Then the sides
were planked up to their total of
sixteen strakes. The massive mast

Cross-section of the Gokstad ship, showing the mast supports and clinker construction. There are no benches, so the oarsmen use their sea chests to sit on.

fish lay on the crossbeams; like that of the Oseberg ship, it was slotted to allow the mast to be raised and lowered. The deck planks, laid across the crossbeams, were loose and could be lifted to stow items below deck or to bail water.

The ship was steered by a massive oar lashed to a boss projecting from the stern quarter. It could be lifted when the ship sailed in shallow water or ran up on a beach. The ship also had sixteen pairs of conventional pine oars graduated in length so that they would all strike the water at the same time. As there were no seats for the oarsmen, it has been conjectured that they sat on the sea chests that held their personal belongings.

The exact details of the Gokstad rigging are not known. The mast did not survive intact, but it is estimated to have been between 10 m and 13 m (33 to 43 ft.) high. A mass of red and white fabric found in the ship was probably the sail. Unfortunately, it could not be preserved. The sail hung from a horizontal yard about 11 m (37 ft.) long. When the sail was not in use, it and the yard rested in T-shaped cradles that stood on deck.

Shields painted alternately yellow and black were fastened along the sides of the Gokstad ship, one to each oar. These were probably only displayed when the ship was at anchor, as they covered the oarports and would have prevented the oars being used. It is possible that they were displayed while the ship was under sail, but they could easily have been torn away by a large wave.

The Gokstad ship was supremely seaworthy; its design compares favourably with that of a modern racing yacht. Several replicas have been built, and they all proved to be fast, trustworthy vessels. The most accurate replica, built by Captain Magnus Andersen of Norway, was sailed to Chicago for the 1893 Columbian Exposition. It can still be seen in Lincoln Park, Chi-

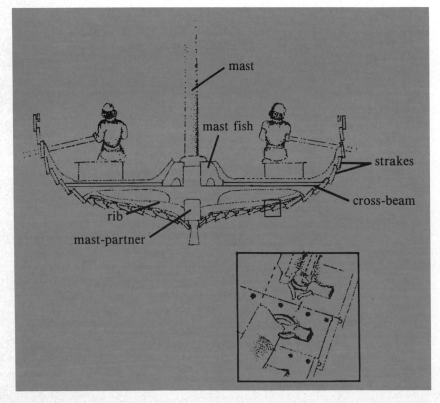

mast fish

strakes

cross-beam

rib

mast-partner

Ships and Shipbuilding

Viking ships from Oseberg and Gokstad, Norway. The two large ships would have been used by aristocrats for travelling with their retainers. The small boat was used for fishing and general transportation.

The long, lean Gokstad ship is a splendid example of a Viking warship. Fast and manoeuvrable, propelled by either sail or oars, such a ship would seldom be at the mercy of wind or tide.

Other traces of Viking warships have been found at Skuldelev and Ladby in Denmark. The Ladby ship survived only as a shadow in the soil. All the wood had rotted, but the rivets that joined the planks had remained in place. By careful excavation, it was possible to reconstruct the ship, and replicas have been built and sailed by Danish Scout troops.

cago. Captain Andersen was very enthusiastic about the sailing qualities of his ship, and with good reason. It left Norway on April 30 and, after a stormy crossing, arrived safely in Newfoundland on May 27. The ship was extremely flexible, and the edges sometimes twisted as much as 15 cm (6 in.) out of true. This enabled it to ride lightly over the waves, conforming to their shape, rather than smashing rigidly through them.

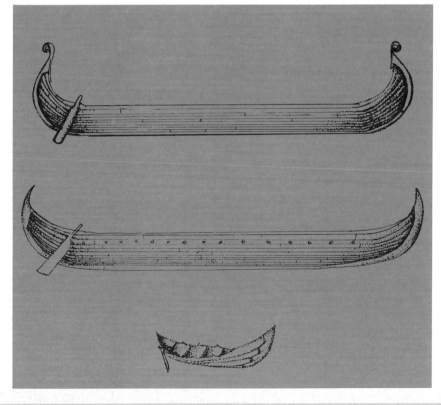

However, not all Viking ships were warships. The most common vessel was a small skiff between 5 and 6 m (15 to 20 ft.) long. (Three were found in the Gokstad burial, where they served as ships' boats.) Primarily rowboats, with four or six oars, they were used for fishing and transportation in coastal regions. Small boats of this type are still being built in parts of Norway and in the Shetland and Faroe Islands, with very few modifications.

About the year 1000 A.D., five ships were sunk in the Roskilde fiord near Skuldelev, Denmark, in order to blockade the channel and protect the city of Roskilde. The ships were excavated in 1962 by building a dam around the area and pumping out the water. After painstaking excavation and conservation, the five ships were reassembled at the Viking Ship Hall in Roskilde. Two are warships, similar to the Gokstad ship. One is 18 m (59 ft.) long, but the other is a giant. It is at least 28 m (92 ft.) long, and may be longer once reconstruction is complete. A third ship found at the site seems to have been a ferry or a small fishing boat. It was about 12 m (40 ft.) long and 2.5 m (8 ft. 2 in.) wide.

The larger merchant ship from Skuldelev
with a full cargo. This type of ship crossed
the Atlantic to Iceland, Greenland, and
North America.

However, the most interesting find at Skuldelev were two cargo ships of the type used by Viking merchants and colonists. The smaller of the two is 13.5 m (43 ft.) long and 3.2 m (10 ft.) wide; the larger is 16.3 m (53 ft. 5 in.) long and 4.6 m (15 ft.) wide. They differ from the warships in several important respects. They are primarily sailing ships, and lack the row of oar-ports characteristic of warships. There are only a few oar-holes in the bow and stern of each ship, presumably to help the ship come alongside quays and to push the stem and stern around into the wind. Moreover, the cargo ships are much shorter, broader, and deeper than warships. The cargo ships would have provided greater resistance to the lateral pressure of the wind, and were better able to sail to windward, that is, they could sail at an angle to the wind instead of just being blown along by it.

Because these ships did not need oars and oarsmen, more room was available for cargo. To increase the cargo space, the middle of the boat was left open; only the bow and stern were decked over for the crew. Thus, the ship could be loaded with horses, cattle, sheep, barrels of wine, and imported goods, and the whole cargo covered with cloth or hides to keep it dry. These ships, not the sleek warships, enabled the Vikings to conquer the North Atlantic, settle in Iceland and Greenland, and finally set foot on the shores of North America.

The Norse in North America

Robert McGhee

The tenth-century Norse expansion across the North Atlantic brought Eiric the Red to Greenland in about 982 A.D. Within a decade, Norse farms were established along the shores of the west Greenland fiords. During the next four centuries, ships from Greenland, Iceland, and northern Europe criss-crossed the North Atlantic, bringing immigrants to the new colonies, taking visitors to the Old Country, and transporting the vital trade goods on which the Greenlandic colonies depended for their livelihood.

The settlements on the west coast of Greenland were only eight hundred kilometres from the Labrador shore and less than five hundred kilometres – a little more than two days' sailing – from Baffin Island. The Norse were excellent seamen, and their ships were capable of extended ocean voyages; yet the accounts of the time tell numerous stories of ships being driven far from their routes by storms. Norse navigators did not have the compass, and celestial navigation was often impossible due to clouds or the bright nights of the northern summer. Ships often survived storms only by running before the wind for days on end. It was, therefore, almost inevitable that

North America would be discovered by ships being driven off course between Greenland and the Old World.

Such an event seems to have taken place about 986 A.D., only a few months after Eiric returned from Iceland with the first Greenlandic colonists. Our knowledge of this event, and of the voyages that it instigated, comes entirely from the Icelandic sagas, which were preserved in oral tradition until written down during the later mediaeval period. According to these sagas, a skipper named Bjarni Herjolfsson arrived in Iceland from Norway. Upon learning that his family had followed Eiric to

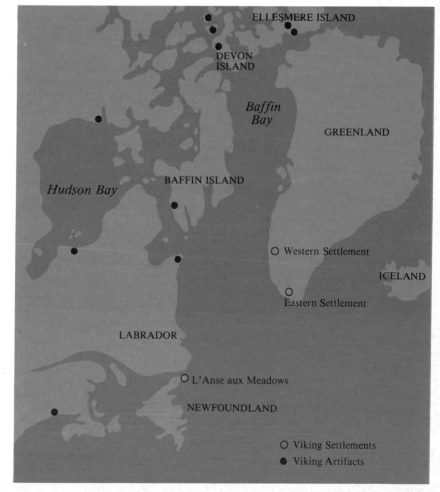

ELLESMERE ISLAND

DEVON ISLAND

Baffin Bay

GREENLAND

Hudson Bay

BAFFIN ISLAND

○ Western Settlement

ICELAND

○ Eastern Settlement

LABRADOR

○ L'Anse aux Meadows

NEWFOUNDLAND

○ Viking Settlements
● Viking Artifacts

Greenland, he decided to continue his voyage to the new settlement, even though he must have had only the vaguest of sailing directions. Three days out from Iceland, his ship was beset by north winds and fog for several days. When the fog cleared, he sailed west; a day later, he sighted a low forested coast. Knowing it could not be Greenland, he headed north and sailed for two days before turning toward shore. The coast was low and wooded. Bjarni continued north for three more days before sighting a rocky, mountainous country that, in his opinion, was good for nothing. Without going ashore, he sailed from the coast and, four days later, made landfall in western Greenland.

The tale of Bjarni's adventure, as told in *The Greenlanders' Saga*, fits well with the geography of eastern North America and with the speed of Norse sailing ships, which probably averaged about two hundred kilometres per day. The first two lands he sighted were almost certainly the forested coasts of Labrador; the mountainous country was either the Torngat Mountain region of northern Labrador or Baffin Island.

Although there must have been considerable interest in the new land to the west, no further exploration seems to have been undertaken for about fifteen years.

Shortly after 1000 A.D., however, Eiric the Red's son Leif bought Bjarni's ship and followed Bjarni's circuit in reverse. He first sighted a mountainous land with glaciers and rocks running down to the coast. He landed and named it *Helluland* or "Flat Stone Land," an apt description of either eastern Baffin Island or the northern regions of Labrador. Continuing south, he discovered a low, wooded coast with extensive beaches of white sand. Leif named this *Markland* or "Wood Land," an appropriate description for the Labrador coast to the south of Hamilton Inlet. Two days to the south, he discovered a third land with good grazing, wood, and even grapes. Leif named the country *Vinland* or "Wine Land." After wintering and doing some exploring, he and his crew took on a cargo of grapes and timber and sailed for Greenland, where there was much discussion of his discoveries.

During the following decade, four voyages set out from Greenland to explore and settle in the new country. The first was led by Leif's brother Thorvald, who spent at least two winters in Leif's houses and explored the neighbouring coasts before being killed by an arrow in a skirmish with the native *Skraelings* of Markland. The following year, another brother, Thorstein, set out to bring home

Thorvald's body, and, probably, to explore further. His ship was storm-tossed for the entire summer, and he never sighted land. He arrived back in Greenland only to die there the following winter.

The next and largest expedition was led by an Icelander, Thorfinn Karlsefni, who had married Thorstein's widow. Karlsefni's three ships carried approximately 160 men, several with their families, livestock, and other necessities for founding a permanent colony. In the course of their explorations during their three years in Vinland, they traded goods for native furs. Eventually, however, relations with the native Skraelings turned hostile. There were two battles and, probably as a result of this opposition, the Norse decided to abandon their colony and to return home.

The final expedition took place the following year, led by Eiric's daughter Freydis and two Icelandic brothers. During the crew's first winter in Vinland, a murderous feud broke out between the Greenlandic and Icelandic factions, and the survivors rapidly withdrew to Greenland.

This expedition seems to have been the last Norse voyage of exploration, and there are no further references to Vinland in the Icelandic sagas. Although there were probably no further attempts at colonization, it seems likely that ships occasionally might have ventured westward from Greenland to cut

The only missing feature in this location of Vinland is the wild grapes for which Leif named the country. It has been suggested that Leif's grapes were one of the many varieties of abundant berries, from which Newfoundlanders still make palatable wines. However, in the

comparatively warm period of the Vinland voyages, grapes may have grown in the region. In fact, Cartier reported wild grapes growing on the shores of the St. Lawrence five centuries later. Perhaps the most telling comment on the

timber from the forests of Markland or to trade with the Skraelings. Two brief records of such voyages have been preserved in Icelandic annals. One states that in 1121 A.D. Bishop Eiric of Greenland went in search of Vinland. Nothing else is known of this Eiric, and there are no records of the Greenlanders having a bishop until several years later, so this account may be suspect. The second states that, in the year 1347 A.D., a small Greenlandic ship on a voyage to Markland was blown eastward to Iceland.

Scholars and enthusiasts alike have argued for years about exactly where Vinland was. The saga descriptions are too vague to place the colony accurately, and a case for locations as diverse as Labrador, Florida, the Great Lakes, and Hudson Bay has been put forward. However, most scholars feel that the geographical descriptions and sailing distances recorded in the sagas best fit northern Newfoundland. Supporting evidence is found in the Sigurdur Stefansson map. This is an Icelandic chart of the late sixteenth century, showing Greenland, Helluland, Markland, and the *Promontorium Winlandiae*, which closely matches the great northern peninsula of Newfoundland in both shape and latitudinal position.

The Norse settlement site at L'Anse aux Meadows, Newfoundland. The site consists of three groups of houses and a smithy, located on the shore of Black Duck Brook. (Photo: Parks Canada)

grapes comes from Thorhall the Hunter, a disgruntled member of Karlsefni's crew, who composed a poem comparing the legendary wine and plentiful food of Vinland with the spring water and whale meat that he found in the new land.

Most scholars concede that only archaeological evidence can confirm the location of Vinland. In 1960, the first and only widely accepted Norse site in North America was discovered at L'Anse aux Meadows on the northern tip of Newfoundland. Here, in a grassy meadow facing north across the Strait of Belle Isle to the Labrador coast, archaeological

crews from Scandinavia and Canada unearthed the remains of eight sod-walled structures similar to those built by the Norse in Iceland and Greenland. Three are large, multi-roomed dwellings; others are smaller buildings, and one housed a forge or smithy.

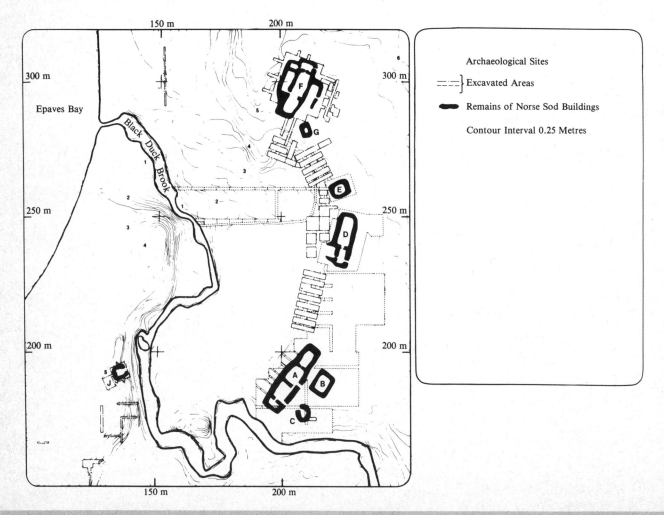

Archaeological Sites

===} Excavated Areas

Remains of Norse Sod Buildings

Contour Interval 0.25 Metres

Reconstruction of the turf houses built by the Norse at L'Anse aux Meadows. (Photo: J. Steeves, Parks Canada)

Spindle whorl found at L'Anse aux Meadows. As spinning was women's work, this spindle whorl may indicate that there were women in the first Norse settlement in North America. (Photo: Parks Canada)

Bronze ringed pin found at L'Anse aux Meadows. Cloak pins like these were fashionable in the Viking settlements in Scotland, Ireland, and Iceland. (Photo: Parks Canada)

Excavations in the buildings and the surrounding meadows and bogs have produced more than one hundred artifacts associated with the European occupation, including a soapstone spindle whorl, a stone lamp, a bronze ring-headed pin, a bone pin, many iron nails or rivets, a sewn birch-bark container, the floorboards of a boat, and several other wooden pieces. Radiocarbon dating indicates that the site was used by various groups over several millennia, but that it was primarily occupied about the time of the Vinland voyages. The absence of a midden of bones and other debris, as well as the fact that none of the houses was rebuilt or underwent major repairs, indicates that the main occupation lasted for at most a few years.

In sum, the archaeological evidence indicates that L'Anse aux Meadows was occupied briefly by Europeans several centuries before Columbus's discovery of America, and it seems most likely that this occupation was by the Greenlandic Norse. Archaeology has not proven that this site was the Vinland of the sagas – it may have been built and occupied by an unrecorded Norse expedition – but it is in the most likely geographical area, and the remains left by the brief visits of Leif, Karlsefni, and the others would probably look very much like those found at L'Anse aux Meadows.

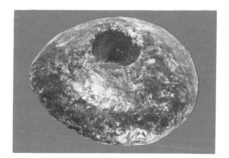

Eleventh-century Norwegian penny found on a native American site in Maine. (Photo: Maine State Museum)

All other verified Norse archaeological finds in North America have come from Indian and Eskimo settlements. The people who occupied these sites were the Skraelings of the sagas. Only recently has archaeology been able to suggest who these Skraelings were. At the time of the *Vinland* explorations, the native peoples of northeastern North America were also engaging in population movements. The Norse may have come in contact with three distinct groups at different times and in different places. The Dorset Palaeoeskimos, an Eskimo or Eskimo-like people, had long occupied the Arctic, but were about to be displaced by the ancestors of the present Eskimos. The Archaic Indians were the ancestors of the Montagnais of Labrador and the Beothuk of Newfoundland. The Thule Eskimos were expanding rapidly eastward from their Alaskan homeland and reached Greenland about the same time as the Norse.

For a thousand years before the Norse voyages, the Dorset people had occupied coastal Labrador and Newfoundland, and the remains of their camps have been found at L'Anse aux Meadows. By the time the Norse journeyed to Vinland, however, the Dorsets had abandoned Newfoundland and southern Labrador, although they continued to occupy northern Labrador and

Baffin Island – the Helluland of the sagas. Their place in the south had been taken by Indians, who also left archaeological remains at L'Anse aux Meadows. These must have been the Skraelings with whom the Norse traded and fought in Vinland and Markland.

A recent archaeological find from an Indian site on the coast of Maine represents the only known Norse object from good archaeological context to have been discovered south of L'Anse aux Meadows. This find hints that there was contact among the Norse, Dorset, and Indian peoples at least half a century after the Vinland voyages. The object is a small, silver coin minted in Norway between 1065 A.D. and 1080 A.D., during the reign of Olaf Kyrre. There is no evidence that the Norse visited the area, but it is possible to trace how the coin may have reached the site.

Many of the stone tools used by the Indian occupants of the site are made of chalcedony from the Bay of Fundy region to the north. This indicates trade contacts with the north. Moreover, some of the stone tools are made from a type of chert found only in the Ramah Bay region of northern Labrador, an area occupied at the time by the Dorset people. One of the tools is a polished chert artifact of a type made only by the Dorsets. This indicates that trade networks extended north from Maine to Indian groups in the Maritime Provinces and Labrador. These people, in turn, traded with the Dorset Palaeoeskimos of the far north. The Labrador Dorsets were probably in contact with their relatives on the eastern Arctic Islands. It is entirely likely that, here or in Labrador, the Dorsets traded or fought with the crew of a Norse ship and obtained the coin that eventually ended up in Maine, perforated to be worn as an amulet.

A second Norse artifact, a small piece of smelted sheet copper reworked to form an amulet, was found in a twelfth-century Dorset site on the east coast of Hudson Bay. This, too, seems to indicate contact between the Norse and Dorset people and subsequent trade of Norse objects through the native exchange networks.

The remaining Norse artifacts discovered in North America have come from Eskimo sites in Arctic Canada. When Eiric the Red discovered Greenland, he found it unoccupied, although the remains of houses, boats, and stone tools – almost certainly left by the Dorset people – indicated previous occupation. However, about the same time the Norse began to colonize the fiords of southwestern Greenland, the Eskimos, who had been expanding eastward from Alaska, crossed from Ellesmere Island to occupy the northwestern regions of the country. The first recorded contact between the two groups took place in 1266 A.D. A Norse hunting expedition to the Disco Bay area, far to the north of the main colonies, encountered traces of the Eskimos. A second, probably contemporary, reference states that the hunters had discovered small people in the north. These Skraelings had no iron, but used weapons of walrus ivory and knives of stone.

During succeeding generations, the Eskimo population expanded southward down the coast; but, although contact between the two races must have occurred frequently, there are only two references in historical sources. One, dating from about 1350, states that the Western Settlement, the more northerly of the two Norse colonies, had been abandoned and was in the hands of the Skraelings. The second reference records that about 1418 the Eastern Settlement had been attacked "from the nearby shores of the heathens," and that most of the churches had been burned.

Recent archaeological finds suggest that contacts between the Norse and the Eskimos may have occurred earlier, and may have been more frequent and extensive than European historical accounts record. Most of these are finds of European artifacts and materials in Thule Eskimo archaeological sites.

The largest number of objects has come from sites on the central east coast of Ellesmere Island. This part of Canada is separated from northwestern Greenland by only fifty kilometres of water or ice. Here pieces of chain mail, woollen cloth, oak, iron rivets, fragments of coopered barrels or tubs, and small pieces of iron and copper have been found in Eskimo winter houses. A series of radiocarbon tests dating these sites and others in the adjacent area of northwestern Greenland are rather confusing. The dates range from the tenth to the fifteenth centuries A.D., but the average date is the mid-thirteenth century, about the time that historical records first mention contact between Eskimos and Norse.

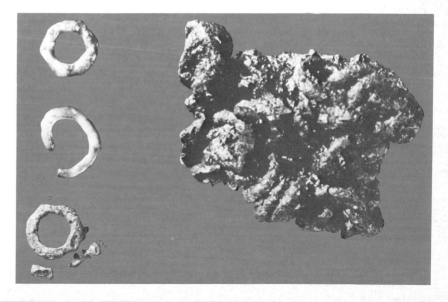

Iron rivets found on a Thule Eskimo site on
Ellesmere Island.

Fragment of a bronze bowl from a Thule
Eskimo site on Devon Island.

Other sites containing Norse material, however, seem to date earlier. On the west coast of Hudson Bay, a piece of smelted iron, probably obtained through inter-group trade from Eskimos to the North and East, dates from the late twelfth or early thirteenth century.

Small pieces of smelted copper, bronze, and iron have been found in other Thule Eskimo sites, and it appears that Norse materials were widely distributed throughout the Eskimo populations of Arctic Canada. One can assume that much of this distribution occurred through trade among Eskimo groups, but how the Eskimos came into possession of the material in the first place is still unknown.

All the sites mentioned above predate the historical accounts of Eskimos reaching the area of Norse settlement in southwestern Greenland. From the eleventh to the mid-fourteenth centuries, the only Norse who were likely to have come in contact with Eskimos were hunters. Each summer, Norsemen travelled five hundred kilometres or more north of the main colonies to hunt seal, walrus, and bear in the Nordsetur region, the central west coast of Greenland, and, perhaps, even farther north. The summer hunt was very important to the Greenlandic economy; walrus hides, ivory, bearskins, and even live bears from the Nordsetur were the primary trade goods that the Greenlandic Norse sent to Europe in exchange for grain, metal, timber, and other necessities that had to be imported.

On such expeditions, small parties of hunters may have encountered Eskimo groups; in experience and equipment, these Eskimos would have been roughly equal to the Norse in fighting or trading. In one or more skirmishes between such groups, the Eskimos may have acquired much of the material now being found in the Canadian Arctic archaeological sites. On the other hand, Vinland sagas tell us that the Norse were willing to trade with the Skraelings, and these particular Skraelings must have had skins and ivory that the Norse required. They may have exchanged these valuables for small pieces of metal or worn-out tools, establishing a more or less regular trade profitable to both sides.

Arm from a bronze balance scale found on a Thule Eskimo site on Ellesmere Island.

Wooden figurine carved by Thule Eskimos, depicting a Norseman in thirteenth-century costume with a crucifix on his chest.

Two recently discovered objects hint that the Eskimos of Arctic Canada did not receive all of their European material through long-distance trade; they may actually have met sailors or traders from Greenland. One artifact, found in a fourteenth-century Eskimo site on the west coast of Ellesmere Island, is characteristic of mediaeval European traders; it is part of a folding bronze balance used for weighing coins and other small objects. It may have been captured from a Norse party in Greenland, but such balances are fairly rare, and none has been found in any of the Norse settlements so far excavated in Greenland. It seems unlikely that such an artifact would have been carried by Norse hunting parties in the Nordsetur, and it suggests that this far northern region may have been visited by a trader looking for skins or ivory.

The second object is a small wood carving recovered from a thirteenth-century Eskimo house in southern Baffin Island, the Helluland of the sagas. The carving is done in characteristic Thule Eskimo style, but it depicts a person dressed in what seems to be European clothing with what appears to be a cross on the chest. Although there is no mention of Helluland after the Vinland voyages in historical records, we know that the Greenlandic Norse made at least occasional journeys to Markland until the mid-fourteenth century.

We also know that the most likely route to Markland was past the shores of Helluland, southeastern Baffin Island. The Eskimo carver seems to have met someone dressed in European clothing – perhaps a sailor on his way to Labrador for a shipload of timber or a trader who came ashore on Baffin Island to exchange metal scraps for skins and ivory.

Rather tenuous evidence exists of Norse visits to the northern coast of Ungava, just across Hudson Strait from the site where the carving was found. It has been suggested that a number of large stone cairns in Ungava were built by the Norse. Most of the structures are of Eskimo construction, and no identifiable Norse artifacts have been found in the region; nonetheless, the cairns are not of the type usually built by the Eskimos. Ungava is within the range of Norse exploration and, perhaps, trading; and it is possible that future archaeology will uncover evidence that the cairns were built by Greenlandic visitors.

There are no further indications of a Norse presence in the New World. Unfortunately for those who would like to believe that much of the continent was explored or settled by Norse Vikings, archaeology confirms only what common sense and the sagas tell us. Nonetheless, enthusiasts have produced a widespread scattering of forged runic inscriptions, faked or planted Norse objects, and misinterpreted structures found across much of North America and as far south as Paraguay.

The Norse did discover North America, but their exploration and settlement were limited to a few tentative attempts along the northeastern coasts of Canada and, perhaps, in the eastern Arctic regions closest to and most closely resembling their North Atlantic homelands. Here, for the first time in their westward expansion, they discovered regions already populated by peoples who outnumbered the small exploring or colonizing parties that could be carried by Norse ships.

When Thorvald Eiricson's party met and fought with the Indians of Labrador, human occupation had, for the first time, completed its spread around the earth. It was probably this fact above all others that prevented further Norse expansion into the New World.

None of these finds proves that the Norse knew of Arctic Canada as anything more than the barren and unoccupied Helluland of the sagas. The Eskimos of the region must have known of the Norse, however, at least through vague stories passed along the trade networks with the materials originating in the colonies in Greenland. If the Norse did visit the area fortuitously – as a stop on their wood-gathering expeditions to Labrador – or to trade with the Eskimos, such visits probably would have been irregular and brief. Therefore, the Norse would have had little influence on the country or its inhabitants. After the mid-fourteenth century, the loss of the Western Settlement, a worsening climate, declining trade with Europe, and the increasing scarcity of seaworthy ships would have ended even this limited contact with North America.

Gold bracteate. The man's face in the centre of the bracteate is derived from the portraits of emperors on Roman coins. Sixth century

Bird-shaped mounts from an aristocrat's
grave on Gotland.
Seventh century

Sixth-century brooch, used to fasten a cloak
or shawl about the shoulders.
Sixth century

Bronze statuette of Frey, god of fertility.
Tenth century

Viking sword. The hilt is encrusted with
silver, copper, and brass.
Ninth century

Gold collar made of hollow tubes ornamented with filigree and granulation.
Sixth century

Gilt-bronze weather-vane that once flew
from the prow or the mast of a Viking ship.
Ribbons or small chains would have been
fastened through the holes in the edge of
the vane to indicate the speed and direction
of the wind.

Viking head carved in elk antler.
Eleventh century

Sixth-century grave mounds at Gamla Uppsala, Sweden.
(Photo: Kate Gordon)

List of Artifacts

I. Grave Groups

Migration Period
(400 A.D. – 550 A.D.)

1. Grave find, male
   Viken, Lovö, Uppland
   Fifth century
   SHM 29401:3

   Scabbard chape, silver and
   niello
   H. 4.0 cm

   Miniature chape, gilt silver
   H. 2.1 cm

   Two strap mounts, gilt
   bronze
   L. 4.0 cm

   Ornamental button, gilt silver
   D. 1.8 cm

   Clasp button, gilt silver
   D. 1.0 cm

   Sleeve clasp, bronze
   L. 2.8 cm

   Lance head, iron
   L. 49.5 cm

   Twenty playing pieces, antler
   D. 1.2 cm – 1.7 cm

2. Grave find, female
   Ekeryd, Söderåkra, Småland
   Fifth century
   SHM 27781

   Two brooches, bronze
   L. 6.9 cm and 4.5 cm

   Dress pin, bronze
   L. 4.0 cm

   Twenty-three beads as
   necklace, amber
   D. 0.4 cm – 1.5 cm

3. Grave find, probably female
   Brucebo, Väskind, Gotland
   Fifth century
   SHM 11351:9   Nine items

   Pendant, silver
   L. 1.6 cm

   Brooch, bronze
   L. 4.5 cm

   Sleeve clasp, gilt bronze
   L. 4.1 cm

   Buckle, bronze
   L. 5.5 cm

   Two belt mounts, bronze
   L. 2.8 cm and 3.2 cm

   Three beads, glass

Merovingian Period
(550 A.D. – 800 A.D.)

4. Grave find, female
   Harby, Ljungby, Småland
   Seventh century
   SHM 25151:XI

   Serpent brooch, bronze
   L. 7.5 cm

   149 beads as necklace, glass
   paste

5. Grave find, male
   Vallstenarum, Vallstena,
   Gotland
   Seventh century
   SHM 6295

   Sword hilt, gilt bronze
   L. 13.5 cm

   Two bird-shaped mounts, gilt
   bronze
   L. 8.5 cm

   Four rectangular belt mounts,
   gilt bronze
   L. 9.3 cm

   Four tongue-shaped belt
   mounts, gilt bronze
   L. 11.5 cm

   Five disc-shaped belt mounts,
   gilt bronze
   D. 2.8 cm

   Bridle, reconstructed with
   original mounts, gilt bronze
   H. 66.5 cm

   Shield, reconstructed with
   original studs and mounts
   D. 65.0 cm

Viking Period
(800 A.D. – 1050 A.D.)

6. Grave find, female
   Överhassla, Häggeby,
   Uppland
   Eight century
   SHM 17084

   Four pendants, bronze
   D. 3.8 cm

   Forty beads as necklace,
   glass, bronze

7. Grave find, female
   Othem, Gotland
   Eighth century
   SHM 11887:1

   Nine bracteates, gilt bronze
   D. 3.0 cm – 5.4 cm

   Disc-on-bow brooch, gilt
   bronze with garnets
   L. 13.5 cm

   Animal-head brooch, bronze
   L. 6.5 cm

   Dress pin, bronze

   Buckle, bronze

   Key, bronze
   L. 9.0 cm

   Two necklace spacers and six
   chains, bronze
   H. 4.5 cm

8. Grave find, male
   Vendel, Uppland
   Tenth century
   SHM 7250:9

   Sword, iron
   L. 90.5 cm (two pieces)

   Knife and sheath mounts,
   iron, bronze
   L. 55.0 cm

   Axe, iron
   L. 22.0 cm

   Spearhead, iron
   L. 56.5 cm

   Eighteen arrowheads, iron
   L. 9.0 cm

   Two shield bosses, iron
   D. 15.5 cm

   Saddle mount, iron
   L. 16.5 cm

   Pennannular brooch, iron
   L. 21.3 cm

   Tool with serrated edge
   (horse scraper), iron
   L. 17.1 cm

   Cauldron, iron
   D. 26.0 cm

   Hook, iron

   Link, iron

   Spike, iron

   Two rein guides, gilt bronze
   L. 13.5 cm and 12.0 cm

   Ten strap mounts, bronze on
   leather

   Twenty playing pieces, bone

   Two combs, one with case,
   antler
   L. 11.0 cm and 14.0 cm

   Two whetstones

9. Grave find, female
   Gränby, Äretuna, Uppland
   Ninth or tenth century
   SHM 28402

   Two oval brooches, bronze
   L. 10.9 cm

   Equal-armed brooch, bronze
   L. 8.7 cm

   Two armrings, bronze
   D. 7.5 cm

   Twenty-three beads as necklace, rock crystal, cornelian,
   glass

II. Industry and Trade

Craftsmen and Merchants at Birka

Bone and antler working

10. Grave find, female
Norrkvie, Grötlingbo,
Gotland
Ninth century
SHM 27739

    Drum-shaped brooch, bronze
    D. 6.2 cm

    Two animal-head brooches,
    bronze
    L. 5.7 cm

    Buckle with three chains,
    bronze
    D. 3.8 cm

    Armring, bronze
    D. 5.0 cm

    Two comb handles, bronze
    L. 11.9 cm

    Key, bronze
    L. 9.0 cm

    Ball-headed pin, bronze,
    silver
    L. 7.75 cm

    Two necklace spacers, bronze

    Nineteen mitre-shaped
    pendants, bronze

    103 beads as four strings,
    glass, amber, calcite

11. Raw material, bone and
antler
Birka, Adelsö, Uppland
Ninth or tenth century
SHM 5208

12. Semi-manufactured handle
and two plates for comb,
antler
L. 10.8 cm, 3.5 cm, and
3.9 cm
Birka, Adelsö, Uppland
Ninth or tenth century
SHM 5208:883, 875

13. Comb, antler
L. 11.2 cm
Birka, Adelsö, Uppland
Tenth century
SHM 5208:736

14. Comb, antler
L. 21.0 cm
Birka, Adelsö, Uppland
Tenth century
SHM 5208:576

15. Spoon, antler
L. 14.3 cm
Birka, Adelsö, Uppland
Ninth or tenth century
SHM 5208:555

16. Five pins, bone, antler
L. 9.7 cm – 17.5 cm
Birka, Adelsö, Uppland
Ninth or tenth century
SHM 5208:995, 997, 976,
987, 1042

17. Dice and three playing pieces,
antler
L. 3.8 cm, D. 1.9 cm –
3.0 cm
Birka, Adelsö, Uppland
Ninth or tenth century
SHM 5208:1728, 1729, 1714,
1708

18. Two skates, bone
L. 20.0 cm and 25.0 cm
Birka, Adelsö, Uppland
Ninth or tenth century
SHM 5208:1640

Amber working

19. Raw material, amber
L. 3.2 cm, 4.2 cm, and
7.7 cm
Birka, Adelsö, Uppland
Ninth or tenth century
SHM 5208:2530

20. Spindle whorl, amber
D. 3.0 cm
Birka, Adelsö, Uppland
Ninth or tenth century
SHM 5208:2010

21. Two playing pieces, amber
D. 2.3 cm and 2.8 cm
Birka, Adelsö, Uppland
Ninth or tenth century
SHM 5208:1765, 1766

22. Ten beads, amber
Birka, Adelsö, Uppland
Ninth or tenth century
SHM 5208:2022

23. Axe-shaped amulet, amber
L. 2.9 cm
Birka, Adelsö, Uppland
Ninth or tenth century
SHM 463:9

24. Pendant, amber
L. 2.9 cm
Birka, Adelsö, Uppland
Ninth or tenth century
SHM 5208:2002

Metal working

25. Crucible, fired clay
L. 6.7 cm
Birka, Adelsö, Uppland
Ninth or tenth century
SHM 5208:2483

26. Moulds for pin and pendant,
shale, clay
L. 5.0 cm and 6.7 cm
Birka, Adelsö, Uppland
Ninth or tenth century
SHM 13838, 5208:2499

27. Hammer and tongs, iron
L. 13.7 cm and 12.2 cm
Ullna, Ö. Ryd, Uppland
Ninth or tenth century
SHM 25848

28. Blank, iron
L. 29.0 cm
Attmar, Medelpad
Ninth or tenth century
SHM 17343

29. Three brooch pins, three
rivets, three knives, iron
L. 5.0 cm – 12.0 cm
Birka, Adelsö, Uppland
Ninth or tenth century
SHM 5208:379, 380, 540,
322, 359

Scales, weights, and currency

30. Scales, bronze
H. 25.0 cm
Blekinge
Tenth century
SHM 3288

31. Five weights, bronze, iron
Hemlinge, Valbo,
Gästrikland
Tenth century
SHM 19802

32. Ten fragments of hacksilver,
silver
L. 2.3 cm – 11.3 cm
Birka, Adelsö, Uppland
Ninth or tenth century
SHM 5208:7

33. Three Arabic coins, silver
Gotland
Tenth century
SHM

(a) Ismā'il ibn Ahmad,
al-Shash, 901-902 A.D.
(b) Ahmad ibn Ismā'il,
Samarqand, 909/910 A.D.
(c) Nasr ibn Ahmad, Samarqand, 922, 923 A.D.

Eastern Imports

34. Pot, clay, Slavic
H. 10.3 cm
Birka, Adelsö, Uppland
Tenth century
SHM Bj 998

35. Pot, clay, copy of a Slavic
type
H. 7.8 cm
Birka, Adelsö, Uppland
Tenth century
SHM Bj 738

36. Fifteen belt mounts adapted
as pendants, silver, probably
Khazarish-Bulgarian
D. 1.3 cm– 3.2 cm
Birka, Adelsö, Uppland
Tenth century
Bj. 606

37. Twenty beads, rock crystal,
cornelian
Birka, Adelsö, Uppland
Ninth or tenth century
SHM 5208:2166, 2031, 2034

38. Strap tag adapted as a
brooch, gilt silver, Frankish
L. 5.1 cm
Birka, Adelsö, Uppland
Ninth century
SHM

39. Three pendant whetstones,
Norwegian
L. 6.3 cm, 7.6 cm, and
10.5 cm
Birka, Adelsö, Uppland
Ninth or tenth century
SHM 5208:2417, 2418, 2420

40. Grave find, female, Baltic
Hugleifs, Silte, Gotland
Eleventh century
SHM 17514
Brooch, bronze
Dress pin, bronze
Neckring, bronze
D. 0.20 cm
Two armrings, bronze

41. Comb pendant, bronze,
Baltic
L. 4.9 cm
Munsö, Uppland
Eleventh century
SHM 479

42. Bird-shaped pendant, bronze,
Russian
L. 5.8 cm
Unna Saiva, Gällivare,
Lappland
Eleventh century
SHM 15721:II 3

43. Pendant, silver, Slavic
L. 3.6 cm
Torsta, Hälsingtuna,
Hälsingland
Tenth century
SHM 6820

44. Ear-ring, silver, Slavic
H. 3.7 cm
Sturkö, Blekinge
Eleventh century
SHM 8770

45. Three mask-shaped pendants,
silver, Slavic or Gotlandic
H. 4.4 cm and 4.6 cm
Fölhagen, Björke, Gotland
Tenth century
SHM 3547

46. Trefoil brooch, bronze,
Frankish
L. 9.3 cm
Småland
Ninth century
SHM 3145

47. Mount, bronze, Hiberno-
Saxon
L. 7.0 cm
Helgö, Ekerö, Uppland
Eighth or ninth century
SHM 27448:7314

48. Thistle brooch, silver,
Hiberno-Scottish
D. 14.0 cm
Bjärnås, Tanum, Bohuslän
Tenth century
SHM 696

Silver hoards

49. Hoard, silver
Vamlingbo/Sundre, Gotland
Tenth century
SHM 881
Two armrings
Two pins for penannular
brooches
Thirty-three spiral rings
Two rods: one stamped, one
of two twisted wires
Five folded rods
Bowl

50. Hoard, silver
Sigsarve, Hejde, Gotland
Eleventh century
SHM 16077, 16200
Three penannular brooches
Three rings for penannular
brooches
Ornamental disc, folded
Ornamental disc, incomplete
Circular dress mount
Support for ornamental disc
"Cordiform" mount
Chain
Chain fastener in shape of
animal head attached to ring
fastener terminal
Ear scoop
Two rim fragments from
different bowls
Scoop handle
Armring
Pin with ring head
Two similar pins
Torc fragment
Portion of three-wire ring
Three bundles of folded wire
Folded wire
Two ribbon-shaped bars
Fragment of a bar

51. Hoard, silver
Mellvigs, Eksta, Gotland
Eleventh century
SHM 13230, 13717, 14478
Two spiral rings of twisted
rods
Spiral ring
Three armlets
Folded rod

III. The Jeweller's Workshop

The Workshop

55. Raw material, crucibles and
    moulds
    Helgö, Ekerö, Uppland
    Sixth or seventh century
    SHM see below

    (a) Three bars, bronze
        SHM 27950:8532,
        28480:9831, 27488:7500
    (b) Sheet metal, bronze
        SHM 25726:3165
    (c) Two sprues, bronze
        SHM 25925:4606,
        25514:2225
    (d) Three crucibles, clay
        SHM 26943:6272,
        27687:8905, 27950:8494
    (e) Clasp-button mould in
        four pieces, clay
        SHM 29094:10993,
        28894:10319, 10663,
        28480:9319

56a. Relief brooch and four clasp
     buttons, gilt bronze, cast
     Nicktuna, Tortuna,
     Västmanland
     Sixth century
     SHM 25334

56b. Mould fragment for lateral
     portion of clasp button, clay
     Helgö, Ekerö, Uppland,
     Sixth century
     SHM 27950

57a. Brooch, gilt bronze with
     white metal reverse, cast
     L. 5.5 cm
     Petsarve, Norrlanda, Gotland
     Sixth century
     SHM 7571:337

57b. Mould fragment and two
     parts of a mould, clay
     Helgö, Ekerö, Uppland
     Sixth century
     SHM 28480, 29094

58a. Brooch, gilt bronze with
     white metal reverse, cast and
     engraved
     L. 10.3 cm
     Sörfors, Attmar, Medelpad
     Sixth century
     SHM 12220

58b. Mould fragment, clay
     Helgö, Ekerö, Uppland
     Sixth century
     SHM 28894

59. Fifteen spiral rings, gold
    Various provenances,
    Uppland
    Fifth century
    SHM (various numbers)

60. Hacksilver from a hoard,
    silver
    Endre, Gotland
    Tenth century
    SHM 1337

Religion

52. Statue of the god Frey,
    bronze
    H. 6.7 cm
    Rällinge, Lunda,
    Södermanland
    Tenth century
    SHM 14232 (copy)

53. Thor's hammer pendant,
    silver and niello
    H. 4.0 cm
    Mikels, När, Gotland
    Eleventh century
    SHM 8578

54. Crucifix, silver
    H. 3.2 cm
    Birka, Adelsö, Uppland
    Tenth century
    SHM Bj 660 (copy)

Casting

61. Brooch in form of
quadruped, bronze, cast with
stamping
L. 5.5 cm
Bjerge, Vallstena, Gotland
Fifth century
SHM 14669

62. Buckle, bronze, cast with
stamping
L. 4.9 cm
Bjers, Hejnum, Gotland
Sixth century
SHM 10298

63. Relief brooch, gilt bronze,
cast with niello, garnets, and
cloisonné
L. 14.5 cm
När, Gotland
Sixth century
SHM 1079

64. Brooch, bronze, cast with
stamping
L. 3.6 cm
Gotland
Sixth century
SHM 10498

65. Brooch, bronze, cast
L. 4.8 cm
Grötlingbo, Gotland
Seventh century
SHM 9325

66. Three dress pins, bronze, cast
L. 9.4 cm, 8.0 cm, and
7.3 cm
Gotland
Seventh or eleventh century
SHM 23849:178, 189, 191

67. Key, bronze, cast
L. 9.7 cm
Salmunds, Levide, Gotland
Eighth century
SHM 9594

68. Key, bronze, cast
L. 10.5 cm
Gårdby, Öland
Ninth century
SHM 3331

69. Pendant in the form of a
man's head, silver, cast
H. 3.0 cm
Aska, Hagebyhöga,
Östergötland
Ninth century
SHM 16560 (copy)

70. Oval brooch, bronze, cast
L. 10.7 cm
Birka, Adelsö, Uppland
Ninth century
SHM Bj 214

71. Oval brooch, gilt bronze with
silver
L. 11.7 cm
Sandby, Öland
Tenth century
SHM 550

72. Equal-armed brooch, gilt
bronze, cast
L. 8.7 cm
Sandby, Öland
Tenth century
SHM 130

73. Disc brooch, gilt bronze, cast
D. 7.5 cm
Annerstad, Småland
Tenth century
SHM 10028

74. Disc brooch, gilt silver, cast
niello
D. 8.4 cm
Jämnö, Gärdslösa, Öland
Tenth century
SHM 13534

75. Trefoil brooch, gilt bronze,
cast
L. 9.1 cm
Sunnäs, Ölme, Värmland
Tenth century
SHM 7878

76. Buckle, gilt silver with
garnets and engraved
interlace
L. 5.2 cm
Sjörup, Häglinge, Skåne
Fifth century
SHM 2457

77. Three strap mounts, bronze,
cast and engraved
L. 8.4 cm, 7.9 cm, and
4.4 cm
Gotland
Seventh century
SHM 7571:523

Plaited wire

78. Two wire torcs, silver, of
four and six strands
D. 29.4 cm
Grönby, Skåne
Eleventh century
SHM 2185

Stamping and punching

79. Two armlets, gold,
    hammered with engraved and
    stamped ornament
    D. 7.1 cm
    Skedemosse, Gärdelösa,
    Öland
    Third century
    SHM 26239

80. Armlet, silver, stamped
    decoration
    D. 6.4 cm
    Havor, Hablingbo, Gotland
    Third century
    SHM 8064:113

81. Four bracteates, gold,
    stamped
    D. 5.0 cm and 2.5 cm
    Fjärestad, Skåne
    Sixth century
    SHM 24624

82. Two bracteates, gold,
    stamped
    D. 3.5 cm and 2.8 cm
    Burlöv, Skåne
    Sixth century
    SHM 2180

83. Two bracteates, gold,
    stamped
    D. 3.0 cm
    Torlunda, Vånga,
    Östergötland
    Sixth century
    SHM 2716

84. Torc, gold, hammered with
    stamping
    D. 17.0 cm
    Tuna, Västerljung,
    Södermanland
    Sixth century
    SHM 13651

85. Torc, gold, hammered with
    stamping
    D. 23.0 cm
    Ryd, Skabersjö, Skåne
    Sixth century
    SHM 13651

86. Armring with four spiral
    rings and one finger-ring
    attached, gold
    D. 8.1 cm
    Hässelby, Algutsrum, Öland
    Fifth or sixth century
    SHM 801

87. Three armlets, silver with
    stamping
    D. 6.7 cm, 6.9 cm, and
    7.5 cm
    Tungelbas, Levide, Gotland
    Tenth or eleventh century
    SHM 16906

Inlaid gems and glass

88. Shield grip, bronze with silver
    and blue glass
    L. 22.0 cm
    Brostorp, Glömminge, Öland
    Second century
    SHM 18964

89. Fibula, silver with blue glass
    L. 8.6 cm
    Havor, Hablingbo, Gotland
    Fourth century
    SHM 8964:136

90. Fibula, gilt silver with red
    and blue glass
    L. 14.9 cm
    Kabbarp, Tottarp, Skåne
    Fourth century
    SHM 11392

91. Foil plaque, gold repoussé
    L. 1.3 cm
    Bolmsö, Småland
    Seventh century
    SHM 14535

92. Two repoussé plaques from a
    drum-shaped brooch with
    filigree and granulation
    L. 3.2 cm x 2.3 cm and
    4.1 cm x 1.6 cm
    Malmsmyr, Rone, Gotland
    Eleventh century
    SHM 16477

Filigree and granulation

93. Two biconical beads, gold
    L. 2.35 cm and 2.05 cm
    Broa, Halla, Gotland
    Second century
    SHM 25378

94. Two pendants, gold
    L. 3.7 cm
    Hörning, Köping, Öland
    Second century
    SHM 3060

95. Collar, gold
    D. 23.0 cm
    Möne, Västergötland
    Sixth century
    SHM 3248

96. Bracteate, gold
    D. 9.2 cm
    Gerete, Fardhem, Gotland
    Sixth century
    SHM 18375

97. Bracteate, gold
    D. 5.2 cm
    Gotland
    Ninth century
    SHM 623

98. Five beads, silver
    D. 2.6 cm and 2.9 cm
    Petes, Öja, Gotland
    Eleventh century
    SHM 792

Cloisonné

99. Neckring, gold, garnet
    cloisonné
    D. 15.5 cm
    Burahus, Ravlunda, Skåne
    Fourth century
    SHM 21528

100. Sword pommel, gold, garnet
    cloisonné
    L. 7.6 cm
    Sturkö, Blekinge
    Sixth century
    SHM 11317

101. Disc-on-bow brooch, gilt
    bronze, garnet cloisonné
    L. 5.9 cm
    Trullhalsar, Anga, Gotland
    Sixth century
    SHM 8555:33

102. Disc-on-bow brooch, gilt
    bronze, garnet cloisonné
    L. 6.7 cm
    Bjers, Hejnum, Gotland
    Seventh century
    SHM 8767:109

103. Disc-on-bow brooch, gilt
    bronze, garnet cloisonné
    L. 6.1 cm
    Allekvia, Endre, Gotland
    Seventh century
    SHM 24277:3

104. Disc-on-bow brooch, gilt
    bronze, garnet and serpentine
    L. 7.1 cm
    Bjers, Hejnum, Gotland
    Seventh century
    SHM 10298:139

105. Necklace spacer, bronze,
    garnet cloisonné
    L. 7.4 cm
    Kunsta, Adelsö, Uppland
    Eighth century
    SHM 18357

Incrustation

106. Spur, iron with bronze, silver
    L. 5.8 cm
    Hörning, Köping, Öland
    Second century
    SHM 14904

107. Sword, iron with silver,
    copper, bronze
    L. 47.0 cm
    Broa, Halla, Gotland
    Ninth century
    SHM 19734:B

108. Sword, iron with silver,
    copper
    L. 99.0 cm
    Kvinneby, Stenåsa, Öland
    Ninth century
    SHM 16646

109. Spearhead, iron with silver
    L. 44.5 cm
    Fornevi, Ockelbo,
    Gästrikland
    Tenth century
    SHM 10694:4

110. Spearhead, iron with silver
    L. 60.0 cm
    Auster, Hangvar, Gotland
    Tenth century
    SHM 2309

Gilding, silver plate, niello

111. Bridle mount, gilt bronze,
silver plate
W. 62. cm
Vennebo, Roasjö,
Västergötland
Fifth century
SHM 6511

112. Disc brooch, bronze with
white metal
D. 3.6 cm
Gråborg, Torslunda, Öland
Seventh century
SHM 1304, 1843:18

113. Strap mount, gilt bronze,
silver plate
L. 7.8 cm
Vallsrum, Runsten, Öland
Sixth century
SHM 1240

114. Bird-shaped brooch, bronze
with white metal
L. 5.9 cm
Hagby, Gärdelösa, Öland
Seventh century
SHM 1304, 1838:142

115. Bird-shaped brooch, bronze
L. 6.9 cm
Möckleby, Öland
Seventh century
SHM 17476

116. Buckle, gilt bronze
L. 8.0 cm
Gotland
Seventh century
SHM 7571:550

117. Drum-shaped brooch, bronze
with silver, gold and niello
D. 6.4 cm
Rotarve, Lye, Gotland
Tenth century
SHM 2829

118. Necklace spacer, gilt bronze
with silver
L. 10.2 cm
Myrände, Arlingbo, Gotland
Eleventh century
SHM 4185

Art styles

119. Relief brooch, gilt silver, cast
and chip carved
L. 14.5 cm
Gräsgård, Öland
Sixth century
SHM 1297

120. Relief brooch, gilt silver,
garnet inlay
L. 21.4 cm
Öland
Sixth century
SHM 16390

121. Relief brooch, gilt silver,
green glass inlay
L. 19.8 cm
Svennevad, Närke
Seventh century
SHM 3445

122. Disc brooch, bronze
D. 4.2 cm
Halla, Gotland
Seventh century
SHM 3653

123. Strap mount, bronze
L. 5.3 cm
Fole, Gotland
Seventh century
SHM 2828

124. Disc-on-bow brooch, gilt
bronze with white metal
L. 16.5 cm
Gumbalde, Stånga, Gotland
Ninth century
SHM 1078:136

125. Chain fastener with five
chains, bronze
H. 7.4 cm
Västös, Hall, Gotland
Ninth century
SHM 3047

126. Animal-head brooch, bronze
L. 5.9 cm
Lundbjärs, Lummelunda,
Gotland
Ninth century
SHM 8807

127. Disc brooch, silver
D. 5.4 cm
Finkarby, Taxinge,
Södermanland
Tenth century
SHM 9136

128. Disc brooch with raised
figures
D. 8.3 cm
Torsta, Hälsingtuna,
Hälsingland
Tenth century
SHM 6820

129. Penannular brooch, gilt
bronze with silver
D. 8.1 cm
Roma, Gotland
Tenth century
SHM 9391

IV. North American Artifacts

130. Scabbard chape, bronze
L. 6.0 cm
Segerstad, Öland
Tenth century
SHM 1304:1845:42

131. Drum-shaped brooch, gilt
bronze, gold
D. 6.4 cm
Pilgårds, Boge, Gotland
Eleventh century
SHM 10654

132. Weather-vane, gilt bronze
L. 37.7 cm
Söderala, Hälsingland
Eleventh century
SHM 15023 (copy)

133. Mount terminating in a
man's head, elk antler
L. 22.0 cm
Sigtuna, Uppland
Eleventh century
SHM 22044 (copy)

Picture stones

134. Picture stone
70.0 cm x 47.0 cm x 10.0 cm
Bopparve, Alva, Gotland
Eighth century
Gotlands Fornsal 10126

135. Picture stone
102.0 cm x 71.0 cm x 18.0 cm
Tängelgårda, Lärbro,
Gotland
Eighth century
SHM 4373

136. Floor board from small boat
36.5 cm x 6.0 cm x 1.0 cm
L'Anse aux Meadows
Parks Canada (copy)

137. Spindle whorl, soapstone
D. 31.0 cm, H. 7.0 cm
L'Anse aux Meadows,
House F
Parks Canada (copy)

138. Lamp, stone
D. 10.0 cm, H. 5.0 cm
L'Anse aux Meadows,
House F
Parks Canada (copy)

139. Nail from bog, iron
8.3 cm x 1.8 cm x 0.7 cm
L'Anse aux Meadows
Parks Canada (copy)

140. Pin, bronze
L. 10.0 cm, H. 0.4 cm
L'Anse aux Meadows,
House A
Parks Canada (copy)

141. Honing stone
7.3 cm x 0.7 cm
L'Anse aux Meadows,
House F
Parks Canada (copy)

142. Carved object found in bog,
function unknown, wood
12.0 cm x 5.3 cm x 4.5 cm
L'Anse aux Meadows
Parks Canada (copy)

143. Carved object found in bog,
function unknown, wood
17.0 cm x 6.5 cm x 2.0 cm
L'Anse aux Meadows
Parks Canada (copy)

144. Iron slag
4.5 cm x 2.5 cm and
4.2 cm x 2.7 cm
L'Anse aux Meadows,
Smithy
Parks Canada

145. Bog iron
L'Anse aux Meadows
Parks Canada

146. Wood chips, with cut marks
from the bog
5.5 cm x 2.4 cm x 1.3 cm;
3.3 cm x 2.1 cm x 0.4 cm;
L. 9.8 cm, D. 0.8 cm
L'Anse aux Meadows
Parks Canada

147. Figurine, wood
5.4 cm x 2.1 cm x 1.0 cm
Baffin Island
National Museum of Man
(copy)

148. Folding balance fragment,
bronze
L. 14.5 cm
Ellesmere Island
National Museum of Man
(copy)

149. Bowl fragment, bronze
10.2 cm x 6.8 cm
Baffin Island
National Museum of Man
(copy)

The copies on display have been
substituted for artifacts too fragile
to be exhibited.

Sources and References

_____. *Westward to Vinland; the Discovery of Pre-Columbian Norse House-sites in North America*. New York: St. Martin's, 1969.

Jones, Gwyn. *A History of the Vikings*. London: Oxford University Press, 1968.

McCartney, A.P., and Mack, D.J. "Iron Utilization by Thule Eskimos of Central Canada." *American Antiquity* 38 (1973):328-38.

Magnusson, Magnus. *Viking Expansion Westward*. New York: H. Z. Walck, 1973.

Musset, Lucien. *Les invasions; le second assaut contre l'Europe chrétienne (VIIe-XIe siècles)*. 2e éd. mise à jour. Nouvelle Clio. Paris: Presses universitaires de France, 1971.

_____. *Les peuples scandinaves au Moyen Âge*. Paris: Presses universitaires de France, 1951.

Olsen, O., and Crumlin-Pedersen, O. *Five Viking Ships From Roskilde Fjord*. Roskilde, Denmark: Viking-eskibshallen, 1978.

Sabo, Deborah, and Sabo, George. "A Possible Thule Carving of a Viking from Baffin Island, N.W.T." *Canadian Journal of Archaeology* 2 (1978): 33-42.

Schledermann, Peter. "Eskimo and Viking Finds in the High Arctic." *National Geographic*, May, 1981, pp. 575-601.

_____. "Notes on Norse Finds From the East Coast of Ellesmere Island, N.W.T." *Arctic* 33(1980): 454-63.

Brøgger, A. W., and Shetelig, Haakon. *Viking Ships: Their Ancestry and Evolution*. London: Hurst, 1972.

Dolley, Michael. "The First Authentic Finding of a Viking-age Coin in Continental America." *Norwegian Numismatic Journal* 2 (1979):23-28.

Foote, Peter G., and Wilson, David M. *The Viking Achievement; The Society and Culture of Early Medieval Scandinavia*. New York: Praeger, 1970.

Graham-Campbell, James. *The Viking World*. New Haven: Ticknor & Fields, 1980.

Harp, Elmer, Jr. "A Late Dorset Copper Amulet from Southeastern Hudson Bay." *Folk* 16-17(1975):33-44.

Ingstad, Anne Stine. *The Discovery of a Norse Settlement in America; Excavations at L'Anse aux Meadows, Newfoundland, 1961–1968*. Oslo: Universitetsforlaget, 1977.

_____. "The Norse Settlement at L'Anse aux Meadows, Newfoundland. A Preliminary Report from the Excavations 1961–1968." *Acta Archaeologica* xli(1970):109-54.

Ingstad, Helge Marcus. *Westward to Vinland: the Discovery of Pre-Columbian Norse House-sites*. London: Jonathan Cape, 1969.

Schonback, Bengt. *Progress Report on Archaeological Fieldwork at L'Anse aux Meadows, June to September, 1974*. Research Bulletin, no. 20. Ottawa: National Historic Parks and Sites Branch, Parks Canada, 1974.

Schonback, Bengt; Wallace, Birgitta; and Lindsay, Charles. *Progress Report on Archaeological Fieldwork at L'Anse aux Meadows, June to October, 1975*. Research Bulletin, no. 33. Ottawa: National Historic Parks and Sites Branch, Parks Canada, 1976.

Skaare, Kolbjorn. "An Eleventh Century Norwegian Penny Found on the Coast of Maine." *Norwegian Numismatic Journal* 2 (1979):4-17.

The Viking. London: Watts, 1966.

Wallace, Birgitta. *The 1976 Excavation at L'Anse aux Meadows, Newfoundland*. Research Bulletin, no. 67. Ottawa: National Historic Parks and Sites Branch, Parks Canada, 1977.

Wilson, David M. *The Northern World; The History and Heritage of Northern Europe, 400–1100 A.D.* London: Thames & Hudson, 1980.

_____. *The Vikings and Their Origins*. New ed. London: Thames & Hudson, 1980.

Wilson, David M., and Klindt-Jensen, Ole. *Viking Art*. Ithaca, New York: Cornell University Press, 1966.